The Music of India

by

H.A. Popley

Revised and Updated by

A.K. Coomaraswamy

Ragani

Low Price Publications

2017

Herbert Arthur Popley (1878-1960)
Ananda Kentish Coomaraswamy (1877-1947)

First Published 1921

Reprinted in **LPP**
1990, 1993, 1996, 2017

ISBN 10: 81-86142-87-8
ISBN 13: 978-81-86142-87-5

Published by
Low Price Publications
A-6, 2nd Floor, Nimri Commercial Centre,
Ashok Vihar Phase 4, Delhi 110052 (INDIA)
tel.: +91-11-27302453 fax.: +91-11-47061936
url: www.LPPindia.com e-mail: info@LPPindia.com

Printed at
D.K. Fine Art Press Pvt. Ltd.
Delhi

PRINTED IN INDIA

This book was originally published in 1921. While we strive to clean and enhance the original work, there are instances where imperfections such as blurred pages, poor pictures or errant marks may have been introduced due to either the quality of the original work or the scanning process itself. Despite these occasional imperfections, we continue to bring this book into print as part of our still-ongoing, initial endeavour of providing customers with access to the best possible historical reprints at the lowest possible prices to suit every pocket. We appreciate your understanding of these occasional imperfections, and sincerely hope you enjoy seeing the book in a format as close as possible to the original work, preserving the historical character of the original artefact.

THE MUSIC OF INDIA

BY

HERBERT A. POPLEY, B.A.

National Council of Young Men's Christian Associations of India, Burma and Ceylon

ASSOCIATION PRESS
5, RUSSELL STREET, CALCUTTA

LONDON : OXFORD UNIVERSITY PRESS
NEW YORK, TORONTO, MELBOURNE,
BOMBAY, CALCUTTA AND MADRAS

J. CURWEN & SONS, LTD., LONDON

PRINTED AT THE
S.P.C.K. PRESS, VEPERY, MADRAS
1921

INTRODUCTORY NOTE

THIS book has been written at the request of the Editors of The Heritage of India Series; and although it has grown beyond the possible limits of that Series and is now published by itself, it still remains, as it was originally planned, a brief introduction to a large and intricate subject. We believe that Indian Music possesses so much value for the life of the people of India that, in this great day of national aspiration and progress, it ought to be known and understood by every man and woman who has India's good at heart, so that it may become cultivated in every city and village throughout the land. The purpose of this book, then, is to provide sufficient information to make insight possible; so that the educated Indian, and also the European, may be stirred to such a living interest in Indian music, both vocal and instrumental, as to start musical societies and schools, and to seek for the wider and more detailed information which this book does not attempt to give.

V. S. DORNAKAL.

J. N. FARQUHAR.

AUTHOR'S PREFACE

No one feels more than the author the deficiencies of this book and the inadequacy of its presentation of a great and living culture. My only real qualification is my love for India, and a keen interest in both the practice and theory of Indian music. This little work is sent out into the world in the hope that it may help to make known the great value of Indian music and that it may play some part, however small, in the improvement and spread of this culture throughout India.

My deepest obligations are to Mr. A. H. Fox Strangways, whose *Music of Hindostan* is the best of the few books which seek to give something like an adequate account of the subject. India can never be too grateful to this musical scholar for the limitless labour, love and imagination he has lavished on Indian music. I have drawn very freely from his book not only accepting many of his ideas as to the development of music both within and without India, but also borrowing a few of his brief definitions and some expository passages of greater length. I owe him a further debt for the large amount of personal help he has given me. He read my manuscript from beginning to end more than once, explained a number of musical difficulties, and, above all, provided the material for the account of the Indian scale, and allowed me to consult him freely while I worked up the material into Chapter III.

I also wish to acknowledge with deep gratitude the large help I have received from a number of friends in India. The following have done so much for me that it is a pleasure to mention their services. Mr. N. V. Bhātkhande, M.A., LL.D., author of a number of musical treatises in Marāṭhī and Hindī, read the draft of the manuscript and suggested many corrections. M. R. Ry. C. R. Śrīnivāsa Aiyengar, B.A., L.T., of the Sanskrit College, Mylapore, gave much assistance with regard to the Sāman chant and ancient books on Indian music; Sāhabzada Syed Sādat Ali Khān Bahādur, Home Secretary of Rāmpur State, who is an accomplished musician, gave many hours of valuable time to satisfy my desire for a better practical knowledge of the music of the north; the Rev. L. I. Stephen of Erode taught me much of what I know, both of theory and practice, in south Indian music; while Takhur M. Nawab Ali Khan of Lucknow rendered valuable help. Thanks are also due to the editors of the Heritage of India series for their kind assistance, and especially to Dr. J. N. Farquhar, who has read through all the proofs with the greatest care and made many suggestions of great value.

To every other one who, whether in conversation or by letter, has given me information or led me to clearer insight I would express my sincere gratitude and thanks.

I wish also to make acknowledgment to the editors of 'Outward Bound' for their permission to make use of the rāga pictures; to the authorities of the Indian Museum, Calcutta, for allowing me the use of valuable negatives for some of the pictures of musical instruments; to the India Office, London, for permission to photograph and reproduce the rāga pictures; and to the proprietors of the *Times of India* for kindly letting me have the use of a number of half-tone blocks of pictures of musical instruments

I also desire to express my thanks to M. Fredalis of Baroda for kind permission to use the half tone block of the Sarangi player, facing p. 108.

May my small book lead many to seek further light on this most interesting part of the wonderful Heritage of India.

I would earnestly ask that readers will not fail to notify me of matters which are open to criticism, or which should be corrected in a subsequent edition.

H. A. POPLEY.

Y.M.C.A., Madras.
April, 1921.

SCHEME OF TRANSLITERATION

Gutturals	k	kh	g	gh	ṅ	
Palatals	ch	chh	j	jh	ñ	ś
Linguals	ṭ	ṭh	ḍ	ḍh	ṇ	sh
Dentals	t	th	d	dh	n	s
Labials	p	ph	b	bh	m	
	y	r	l	v	h	
Anusvara	ṁ					
Visarga	ḥ					

CONTENTS

ILLUSTRATIONS

I know not how thou singest, my master! I ever listen in silent amazement.

The light of thy music illumines the world. The life breath of thy music runs from sky to sky. The holy stream of thy music breaks through all stony obstacles and rushes on.

My heart longs to join in thy song, but vainly struggles for a voice. I would speak, but speech breaks not into song, and I cry out baffled. Ah, thou hast made my heart captive in the endless meshes of thy music, my master!

TAGORE, GITĀNJALI.

Picture of Megh rāga

From Johnson Collection, India Office, London

CHAPTER I

INTRODUCTION

North and South India differ largely in a multitude of things. The north is the land of the fighting races and has the large towns and cities of India with their keen intellectual and commercial life. The south is the land of peaceful villages, nestling among green fields and gardens, inhabited by a conservative and peace-loving people who are contented with a little. The south was far away from the battlefields of Empire until the time of the British; and so has passed through a more peaceful evolution and has clung more closely to the old ways. When the Muhammadan invasions overwhelmed the cities of the North, the sages and seers fled to the forests of the South, where they were safe from harm and were welcomed by the cultured Dravidians.

These differences are reflected in the music of the North and of the South, though we must not commit the mistake of thinking of these as distinct types of music. There is one Indian music, though there are many ways of working it out; and these all group themselves under the Northern and Southern schools. Distinguished as the Northern or Hindustani school and the Southern or Carnatic school, both are yet based on the principles stated in the ancient Sanskrit treatises on music.

The student of India will find in the same way one India which speaks again and again as he travels from North to South. The atmosphere of mystical devotion and of submission to what is looked upon as the divine will is found in all religious hearts; the one treasure-store of legend and story supplies both North and South with heroes and sages; and agriculture and trade, the village and the home, and all the arts, are filled with the same spirit and use practically the same methods throughout India.

It will be seen as we study this subject that, in the same way, there is an underlying unity in the music of India, revealing itself in qualities which mark it off from the music of the West and which exhibit its common heart.

The two schools tend to-day to coalesce into one unified system, a tendency which is fostered by the all-India music conferences which now meet annually, and also by the very considerable borrowing which is taking place in each system from the other.

It may be well to give at the outset brief definitions of a few fundamental terms which must be used in our exposition from the very beginning. Fuller explanations of these will be found in the body of the work and a Glossary of all the musical words and phrases which occur in the book will be found among the Appendices.

SVARA ... ... One of the seven notes of the gamut.
ŚRUTI ... ... An interval smaller than the semi-tone.
ŚUDDHA SVARA ... The fundamental variety of each of the seven notes.
VIKṚIT ... ... A variety of the Śuddha note.
RĀGA ... ... The melody-types which are the bases of Indian musical compositions.
TĀLA ... ... Time measure.
GRĀMA ... ... An ancient mode or scale.
JĀTI ... ... The old name for melody-types.

The wide differences between Indian and western music on the one hand, and the variant terminology which distinguishes northern from southern musical teaching in India on the other, create so many minor difficulties even in simple matters, that it has been thought well to use in this book a modified notation, based on the Indian tonic sol-fa, so that all musical items may be exhibited in one way and the reader may not have to carry several schemes in his head. Its relations and detailed use are set forth in the following tables :—

I. Table of Note Signatures and Nomenclature

1		2	3	4
The Svara Nomenclature.		Semi-tones of the Western scale.	Notation used in this book.	The Southern names.
Shaḍja Tāra	...	C	Ṡ	Shaḍja Tāra.
Śuddha Ni	...	B	N	Kākali Ni.
Komal[1] Ni	...	B♭	n	Kaiśiki Ni. Shaṭśruti Dha
Śuddha Dha	...	A	D	ChatuḥśrutiDha. Śuddha Ni.
Komal Dha	...	A♭	d	Śuddha Dha.
Pañchama	...	G	P	Pañchama.
Tīvra[2] Ma	...	F♯	m	Prati Ma.
Śuddha Ma	...	F	M	Śuddha Ma.
Śuddha Ga	...	E	G	Antara Ga.
Komal Ga	...	E♭	g	Sādhāraṇa Ga. Shaṭśruti Ri.
Śuddha Ri	...	D	R	Chatuḥśruti Ri. Śuddha Ga.
Komal Ri	...	D♭	r	Śuddha Ri.
Shaḍja	...	C	S	Shaḍja.

My southern friends will notice that the northern system of nomenclature has been adopted. It is true that the southern names of the notes, as well as the northern, go back to ancient musical facts, but they have very little meaning to the ordinary musician to-day and are not clear enough to justify their coming into general use throughout India. The northern system, however, is based on a clear principle and will present no difficulty to the southern student.

The Śuddha notes of the northern system are those of the tonal scale, Bilāval, the European Major scale. With the exception of Ma, all the other notes are flats to the Śuddha note. This is quite different from the southern system, where the Śuddha note is the lowest and the others are all sharps. Clearly confusion would be the only result of an attempt to retain both systems, while from all points

1 'flat 2 'sharp

of view the northern method is preferable. As most of the writer's time has been spent in the south, and his first love for the genial south is always his best love, it is not likely that he has been biassed in coming to this decision.

In our second table the smaller intervals of the Indian octave are exhibited. Here a difficulty appears in the southern system, namely, the merging of the notes as shown in the bracketed pairs of the table. We have decided to ask our southern friends to read Shaṭśruti Ri in those cases where it should occur, even though the symbol g is used and so on for all merged notes.

Tīvra means 'sharp' and is shown by capital with superscript plus, in the case of Ni and Ga. In the case of Ni and Ga it is a sharp of one śruti only. In Ma it is a semitonal sharp, and is shown by a small letter.

Tīvratara is a double sharp, a microtone higher than Tīvra, and is indicated by small letter with plus sign.

Komal is a semitonal flat and is indicated by a small letter.

Atikomal is a microtonal double flat, one śruti lower than Komal. It is indicated by a superscript minus sign on the small letter.

The three voice registers are indicated as follows :—

T.........Tāra or higher register, shown thus Ṡ.
O.........Madhya or middle register, shown thus S.
M.........Mandra or lower register, shown thus Ṣ.

The letters T,O,M, are placed at the beginning of the clef to show the register used.

In the staff notation, when it is desired to show a microtonal sharpening or flattening, the sharp or flat sign is placed over the note, as may be seen in the table of śrutis below. It should be noted that there are other systems of nomenclature current in India besides the two mentioned. For instance, one current in Poona calls the Śuddha notes of our system Tīvra and the Tīvra notes Tīvratara. It is not suggested that the notation here adopted is free from difficulties, but after very careful thought it is the best that we have been able to devise for the purpose of this book. Whether it will be found worthy of wider use it is for others to decide.

II. Table of Śrutis

	Sruti Name		Western Note	Sign	Carnatic Name
22.	SHAḌJA TĀRA	...	C	Ṡ	Shaḍja Tāra.
21.	Tīvra Ni	...	$\overset{\sharp}{B}$	N+	
20.	ŚUDDHA NI	...	B	N	Kākali Ni.
19.	Komal Ni	...	B♭	n	Kaiśiki Ni. Shaṭśruti Dha.
18.	Atikomal Ni	...	$\overset{\flat}{B\flat}$	n	
17.	ŚUDDHA DHA	...	A	D	Chatuḥśruti Dha. Śuddha Ni.
16.	Triśruti Dha	...	$\overset{\flat}{A}$	D−	
15.	Komal Dha	...	A♭	d	Śuddha Dha.
14.	Atikomal Dha	...	$\overset{\flat}{A\flat}$	d	
13.	PAÑCHAMA	...	G	P	Pa.
12.	Tīvratara Ma	...	$\overset{\sharp}{F\sharp}$	m+	
11.	Tīvra Ma	...	F♯	m	Prati Ma.
10.	Ekaśruti Ma	...	$\overset{\sharp}{F}$	M+	
9.	ŚUDDHA MA	...	F	M	Śuddha Ma.
8.	Tīvra Ga	...	$\overset{\sharp}{E}$	G+	
7.	ŚUDDHA GA	...	E	G	Antara Ga.
6.	Komal Ga	...	E♭	g	Sādhāraṇa Ga. Shaṭśruti Ri.
5.	Atikomal Ga	...	$\overset{\flat}{E\flat}$	g−	
4.	ŚUDDHA RI	...	D	R	Chatuḥśruti Ri. Śuddha Ga.
3.	Madhya Ri	...	$\overset{\flat}{D}$	R−	
2.	Komal Ri	...	D♭	r	Śuddha Ri.
1.	Atikomal Ri	...	$\overset{\flat}{D\flat}$	r−	
0.	SHAḌJA	...	C	S	Shaḍja madhya.

For time-measure the following notation is adopted, being similar to the European tonic sol-fa system. The complete bar is indicated by long upright lines, the division within the bar by short upright lines, and the smaller divisions within these by double and single dots. The dash indicates a continuation of the previous note. Thus,

| S : R : G : M | S : R. G | S :— |

The time signature will be shown at the beginning or each piece. The beat is called *Aṅga* or *Tāla*; the bar *Vibhāga* and a section of so many vibhāgas an *Āvarta*. The *Āvarta* will be shown by two long upright lines together.

CHAPTER II

LEGEND AND HISTORY

The beginnings of Indian music are lost in the beautiful and fanciful legends of gods and goddesses who were supposed to be its authors and patrons. The goddess Sarasvatī is always represented as the goddess of art and learning, and she is usually pictured as seated on a white lotus with a *vīṇā*, lute, in one hand, playing it with another, a book in the third hand and a necklace of pearls in the fourth.

The technical word for music throughout India is the word *saṅgīta*, which originally included dancing and the drama as well as vocal and instrumental music. The god Śiva is supposed to have been the creator of this threefold art and his mystic dance symbolizes the rhythmic motion of the universe.

In Hindu mythology the various departments of life and learning are usually associated with different *ṛishis* and so to one of these is traced the first instruction that men received in the art of music. Bharata *ṛishi* is said to have taught the art to the heavenly dancers—the Apsarases—who afterwards performed before Śiva. The *ṛishi* Nārada, who wanders about in earth and heaven, singing and playing on his *vīṇā*, taught music to men. Among the inhabitants of Indra's heaven we find bands of musicians. The Gandharvas are the singers, the Apsarases the dancers, and the Kinnaras centaur-like performers on musical instruments. From the name Gandharva has come the title Gāndharva Veda for the art of music.

Among the early legends of India there are many concerning music. The following is an interesting one from them *Adbhuta Rāmāyaṇa* about Nārada *ṛishi*, which combines criticism with appreciation.

Once upon a time the great *ṛishi* Nārada thought within himself that he had mastered the whole art and science of music. To curb his pride the all-knowing Vishṇu took him to visit the abode of the gods. They entered a spacious building, in which were numerous men and women weeping over their broken limbs. Vishṇu stopped and enquired of them the reason for their lamentation. They answered that they were the *rāgas* and the *rāgiṇīs*, created by Mahādeva; but that as a *ṛishi* of the name of Nārada, ignorant of the true knowledge of music and unskilled in performance, had sung them recklessly, their features were distorted and their limbs broken; and that, unless Mahādeva or some other skilful person would sing them properly, there was no hope of their ever being restored to their former state of body. Nārada, ashamed, kneeled down before Vishṇu and asked to be forgiven.

The *Vedic Index* shows a very wide variety of musical instruments in use in Vedic times. Instruments of percussion are represented by the *dundubhi*, an ordinary drum; the *āḍambara*, another kind of drum; *bhūmi-dundubhi*, an earthdrum made by digging a hole in the ground and covering it with hide; *vanaspati*, a wooden drum; *āghāṭi*, a cymbal used to accompany dancing. Stringed instruments are represented by the *kāṇḍa-vīṇā*, a kind of lute; *karkari*, another lute; *vāṇa*, a lute of 100 strings; and the *vīṇā*, the present instrument of that name in India. This one instrument alone is sufficient evidence of the development to which the art had attained even in those early days. There are also a number of wind instruments of the flute variety, such as the *tūṇava*, a wooden flute; the *nāḍī*, a reed flute; *bākura*, whose exact shape is unknown. 'By the time of the Yajur Veda several kinds of professional musicians appear to have arisen; for lute-players, drummers, flute-players and conch-blowers are mentioned in the list of callings.'

That vocal music had already got beyond the primitive stage may be concluded from the somewhat complicated method of chanting the Sāma Veda, which probably goes back to the Indo-Iranian age. These hymns of the Ṛik and Sāma Vedas are the earliest examples we have of words set to music, unless we except the *Zendavesta*, which may have been chanted. The Sāma Veda was sung according to very strict rules, and present day Sāmagaḥs—temple singers of the Sāman—claim that the oral tradition which they have received goes back to those ancient times. A discussion upon the musical character of the Sāman chant will be found in the next chapter. The *Chhāndogya* and the *Bṛihadāraṇyaka Upanishads* (c. 600 B.C.) both mention the singing of the Sāma Veda and the latter also refers to a number of musical instruments.

One of the earliest references to music is found in the grammarian Pāṇini, who was probably alive when Alexander the Great was in Taxila (326 B.C.) In his comments upon the root Nṛit—to dance—he mentions two persons named Śilālin and Kṛiśāśvin as the authors of two sets of *sūtras* on dancing.

A reference to a musical performance, which if it could be accepted as historical would go back further still is found in the *Pāli Piṭaka* (c. 300 B.C.) in which it is said that two disciples of Gautama Buddha (c. 480 B.C.) attended a dramatic performance, which of course would be musical.

The earliest reference to musical theory seems to be in the *Ṛikprātiśākhya* (c. 400 B.C.) which mentions the three voice registers and the seven notes of the gamut. It is interesting to find that just before this time, Pythagoras in Greece (510 B.C.) worked out the musical system of the Greeks.

In the *Rāmāyaṇa* (400 B.C.—A.D. 200) mention is frequently made of the singing of ballads, which argues very considerable development of the art of music. The poem composed by the sage Vālmīki is said to have been sung before King Daśaratha by Rāma and Lakshmaṇa. The author of the *Rāmāyaṇa* often makes use of musical similes. The humming of the bees reminded him of the music of stringed instruments, and the thunder of the clouds of the beating of the *mṛidaṅga*. He talks of the music of the battlefield, in which the twanging and creaking of the bows takes the place of stringed instruments and vocal music is supplied by the low moaning of the elephants. Rāvaṇa is made to say that 'he will play upon the lute of his terrific bow with the sticks of his arrows.' Lakshmaṇa, entering the inner apartments of Sugrīva's harem, hears the ravishing strains of the music of the *vīṇā* and other stringed instruments accompanied by the faultless singing of accomplished vocalists. Rāvaṇa was a great master of music and was said to have even appeased Śiva by his sublime chanting of Vedic hymns.

The *Rāmāyaṇa* also mentions the *jātis*, which seem to have done duty for the *rāgas* in ancient times. They seem to have been seven in number and may perhaps have begun on each of the seven notes of the gamut. Among the musical instruments mentioned the following are the most important: *bherī*, *dundubhi*, *mṛidaṅga*, *paṭaha*, *ghaṭa*, *paṇava*, and *ḍiṇḍima* among the drums; *mudduka* (brass trumpet) and *āḍambara* (clarionet) among wind instruments; a *vīṇā* played either with the bow or with a plectrum, the *vīṇā* being the name for all stringed instruments.[1]

The *Mahābhārata* (500 B.C.—A.D. 200) speaks of the seven *Svaras* and also of the Gāndhāra Grāma, the ancient third mode which is discussed in the next chapter. The theory of consonance is also alluded to.

The *Mahājanaka Jātaka* (C. 200 B.C.) mentions the four great sounds (*parama mahā śabda*) which were conferred as an honour by the Hindu kings on great personages. In these the drum is associated with various kinds of horn, gong and cymbals. These were sounded in front of a chariot which was occupied, but behind one which was empty. The car used to go slowly round the palace and up what was called 'the kettle-drum road.' At such a time they sounded hundreds of instruments so that 'it was like the noise of the sea.' The *Jātaka* also records how Brahmadatta presented a mountain hermit with a drum, telling him that if he beat on one side his enemies would run away and if upon the other they would become his firm friends.

In the Tamil books *Puṟanāṉūṟu* and *Pattupāṭṭu* (C. A.D. 100–200) the drum is referred to as occupying a position of very great honour. It had a special seat called

[1] See *Music in Ancient India*, by C. Tirumalaiya Naidu.

murasukaṭṭil, and a special elephant, and was treated almost as a deity. It is described as 'adorned with a garland like the rainbow.' One of the poets tells us, marvelling at the mercy of the king, 'how he sat unwittingly upon the drum couch and yet was not punished'. Three kinds of drum are mentioned in these books: the battle drum, the judgment drum, and the sacrificial drum. The battle drum was regarded with the same veneration that regiments used to bestow upon the regimental flag in the armies of Europe and the capture of the drum meant the defeat of the army. One poem likens the beating of the drum to the sound of a mountain torrent. Another thus celebrates the virtues of the drummer:

> For my grandsire's grandsire, his grandsire's grandsire
> Beat the drum. For my father, his father did the same.
> So he for me. From duties of his clan he has not swerved.
> Pour forth for him one other cup of palm tree's purest wine.[1]

The early Tamil literature makes much mention of music. The *Paripādal* (c. A.D. 100–200) gives the names of some of the svaras and mentions the fact of there being seven Pālai (ancient Dravidian modes). The *yāḷ* (யாழ்) is the peculiar instrument of the ancient Tamil land. No specimen of it exists to-day. It was evidently something like the *vīṇā* but not the same instrument, as the poet Māṇikkavāchakar (c. A.D. 500–700) mentions both in such a way as to indicate two different instruments. Some of its varieties are said to have had over 1,000 strings. The *Silappadigāram* (A.D. 300), a Buddhist drama, mentions the drummer, the flute player, and the *vīṇā* as well as the *yāḷ*, and also has specimens of early Tamil songs. This book contains some of the earliest expositions of the Indian musical scale, giving the seven notes of the gamut and also a number of the modes and rāgas in use at that time. The names given to the notes are not those current in the present day and are with one exception pure Tamil words *Tivākaram*, a Jain lexicon of the same period, gives quite a lot of information about early Dravidian music. It mentions two kinds of rāgas; complete or heptatonic, and

[1] From *Pura-porul Veṇbā mālai*, Pope's translation.

transilient or hexatonic and pentatonic, which were called respectively *Paṇ* and *Tiram*; it gives the twenty-two śrutis, which it calls *mātra*; the Tamil names of the seven svaras with the equivalent Sanskrit sol-fa initials, (Sa Ri Ga etc.); the seven Dravidian modes called *Pālai*; four kinds of Yāḷ and the names of 29 *Paṇs*, some of which are still found among the primary rāgas of southern India. All this as well as frequent references to the science of music and to musical performances, both vocal and instrumental, in the Tamil books of this and succeeding periods makes it clear that musical culture had reached a high level among the Dravidian peoples of South India in the early centuries of our era.

The later centuries of the Buddhist period (A.D. 300–500) were more fertile in architecture, sculpture and painting than in music. The dramas of Kālidāsa (c. A.D. 400) make frequent references to music and evidently the rajahs of that time had regular musicians attached to their courts. In the *Mālavikāgnimitra* a song in four-time is mentioned as a great feat performed at a contest between two musicians. The development of the drama after Kālidāsa meant the development of music as well, as all Indian drama is operatic. 'The temple and the stage were the great schools of Indian music.'

This was the time when in Europe Pope Sylvester (A.D. 330) and St. Ambrose (A.D. 374–397) began to elaborate musical theory.

The oldest detailed exposition of Indian musical theory which hás survived the ravages of ants and the fury of men is found in a treatise called *Nāṭya Śāstra* or the science of dancing, said to have been composed by the sage Bharata. The date of this book is usually accepted as the early part of the sixth century. It is stated elsewhere that previous to this Bharata had composed the *Nāṭya Sūtra* or Aphorisms on Dancing, but these have not survived. There is only one chapter of the *Nāṭya Śāstra* (ch. 25) which deals with music proper. This contains a detailed exposition of the *svaras*, *śrutis*, *grāmas*, *mūrchhaṇās*, *jātis*. While the principles of his theory are still active in Indian music, the details of his system belong to the past and are not easily intelligible to the present generation. A translation of a portion of this chapter appeared in Mr. Clement's *Introduction to Indian Music*, and there is a complete French translation by Jean Grosset. The latter however is not quite an accurate guide, as it has taken the word *svara*—used by Bharata for the interval and only secondarily for the note above the interval—to refer to the note below the interval. This involves the correction of all his translation of note names.

An inscription found at Kuḍumiyamālai in the Pudukottai State of the Madras Presidency, which seems to belong to the seventh century, has many references to music. It mentions seven *jātis* and a few of the *śrutis* as well as the seven *svaras*. The words '*antara*' and '*kākali*' are found describing respectively the sharp *śrutis* of Ga and Ni, which is one of the peculiarities of the Southern nomenclature to-day. It is suggested that the inscription is really a piece for the Sāmagaḥ to sing and that the peculiar marks on many of the note signs may be intended to indicate points of Sāman singing.[1]

The seventh and eighth centuries of our era in South India witnessed a religious revival associated with the *bhakti* movement and connected with the theistic and popular sects of Vishṇu and Śiva. This revival was spread far and wide by means of songs composed by the leaders of the movement and so resulted in a great development of musical activity among the people generally and in the spread of musical education. The old melodies to which these songs were sung are now lost, though Travancore claims to have preserved some of them in the ancient Travancore *rāgas* such as *Indisa*, *Indalam*, *Pāḍi*, *Puranira*. The beautiful strip of land on the south-west coast of India between the Western Ghauts and the sea, of which Travancore is now a part, was famed in the centuries before Christ for its commercial activities and its tropical products. This was then the homeland of the Chera kingdom which for a considerable period exercised sovereignty over the whole of South India. It was also the

[1] See *Epigraphia Indica*, vol. xxi, pp. 226–37.

home of an ancient Tamil culture which rivalled the Sanskrit culture of the sacred cities of North India. It is, therefore, no wonder that we should find here a flourishing school of music whose traditions have persisted until this day. It is interesting to note that it was about this time that Gregory the Great was developing music in Europe for religious purposes.

The *Nārada Śikshā*, wrongly connected with the name of the great *ṛishi*, was probably composed between the tenth and twelfth century. It shows considerable development upon the *Nāṭya Śāstra* in its *rāga* system and in a number of matters agrees with the Kuḍumiyamālai inscription where that disagrees with the next important treatise, the *Saṅgīta-Ratnākara*. Some scholars think that the *Nārada Śikshā* comes much later than the twelfth century.

The first north Indian musician whom we can definitely locate both in time and place is Jayadeva, who lived at the end of the twelfth century. He was born at Kendulā near Bolpur, where lives to-day the poet laureate of Bengal and modern India. Kendulā still celebrates an annual fair at which the best musical pieces are regularly performed. Jayadeva wrote and sung the *Gīta Govinda*, a series of songs descriptive of the amours of Kṛishṇa, and so belongs to the number of India's lyrical songsters connected with the *bhakti* revival. Though each song has the name of the *rāga* and *tāla* to which it was sung these are not intelligible to-day to Indian musicians. At that time these songs were known as *Prabhandhas*. The *Gīta Govinda* is a charming lyrical composition, as may be realized to some degree in an English translation of it by Sir Edwin Arnold under the name of *The Indian Song of Songs*. In these songs Rādhā pours forth her yearning, her sorrow and her joy and Kṛishṇa assures her of his love.

We come now to the greatest of ancient Indian musical authorities and one who still inspires reverence in the minds of India's musicians. He was called Śārṅgadeva and lived in the former half of the thirteenth century (A.D. 1210–1247), at the court of the Yādava dynasty of Devagiri in the Deccan. At that time the Marāṭhā empire extended to the river Kāveri in the south, and it is probable that Śārṅgadeva had come into contact with the music of the south as well as with that of the north. His work, the *Saṅgīta-Ratnākara* shows many signs of this contact. It is possible that he is endeavouring to give the common theory which underlies both systems. The result is that a great deal of controversy has arisen as to the exact system described in the book and even as to the reading of the *rāgas* which he describes. No scholar has been able to give a thoroughly satisfactory account of these. The work deals with the whole range of musical form and composition and gives a very detailed account of ancient musical theory. It also mentions a number of musical writers between Bharata and the author, but none of their works survive to-day. The fundamental scale (*śuddha rāga*) of Śārṅgadeva is *Mukhārī*, the modern *Kanakāṅgi*, which is the *śuddha* scale of Carnatic music to-day.

The fourteenth and fifteenth centuries are the most important in the development of the Northern school. It was the time of the Muhammadan conquest. Many of the emperors did a great deal to extend the practice of music and most of them had musicians attached to their court. From this time dates the introduction of Persian models into Indian music, and we also find the differentiation of the northern and southern schools becoming more marked. Amīr Khusru was a famous singer at the court of Sultan Allā-ud-dīn (A.D. 1295–1316). He was not only a poet and musician but also a soldier and statesman and was a minister of two of the Sultans. The qavāli mode of singing—a judicious mixture of Persian and Indian models—was introduced by him, and several of our modern *rāgas* are said to have been originated by him. The Sitār, a modification of the *vīṇā*, was probably first introduced by him. There is a story told of a contest between Amīr Khusru and Gopāl Naik, a musician from the court of Vijayanagar. While Gopāl was singing a beautiful composition, Khusru hid under the throne of the king and afterwards imitated all the beauties of Gopāl's melodies and even surpassed them. Muhammadan historians relate that, when the Moghuls completed the conquest of the

Deccan they took back with them to the North many of the most famous Southern musicians, in the same way that they took toll of the Indian architects and sculptors for their new buildings.

The *Rāgataraṅginī*, composed by Lochanakavi, probably belongs to this period. The major portion of this work is devoted to the discussion of a number of songs by a poet named Vidyāpati, who flourished in the fifteenth century at the court of Rāja Śiva Singh of Tirhut. The author also describes the current musical theories of his day and groups the *rāgas* under twelve *thāṭs* or fundamental modes.

The development of the *bhakti* revival in North India and Bengal under Chaitanya (A.D. 1485–1533) was accompanied by a great deal of musical activity, and it was at this time that the popular musical performances, known as Saṅkīrtan and Nagarkīrtan were first started.

The Emperor Akbar (A.D. 1542–1605) was a fervent lover of music and did much for its development. During his reign *rāgas* were considerably modified under foreign influence and, though some of these modifications transgressed the established practice, they were on the whole to the advantage of music and helped to give to Northern music some of its more pleasing characteristics. Durbāri or chamber music was introduced in the time of Akbar, and from that time developed side by side with the music of the temple and the drama.

Haridās Swāmī was a great Hindu saint and musician who lived at Brindāban, the centre of the Kṛishṇa cult on the banks of the Jumna, in Akbar's reign. He was considered one of the greatest musicians of his time. Tān Sen, the celebrated singer of Akbar's court, was one of his pupils. Many interesting stories are told of Tān Sen, whose name is still fragrant throughout India and 'like whom there has been no singer for a thousand years.' One of these tells how the Emperor after one of his performances asked him if there was anyone in the world who could sing like him. Tān Sen replied that there was one who far surpassed him. At once the Emperor was all anxiety to hear this other singer and when told that he would not even obey the command of the Emperor to come to court, he asked to be taken to him. It was necessary for the Emperor to go in disguise as the humble instrument-carrier of his singer. They came to the hermitage of Haridās Swāmī on the banks of the Jumna, and Tān Sen asked him to sing but he refused. Then Tān Sen practised a little trick and himself sang a piece before his old master, making a slight mistake in doing so. The master at once called his attention to it and showed him how to sing it properly, and then went on in a wonderful burst of song, while the Emperor listened enraptured. Afterwards, as they were going back to the palace, the Emperor said to Tān Sen, 'Why cannot you sing like that?' 'I have to sing whenever my Emperor commands', said Tān Sen, 'but he only sings in obedience to the inner voice.'

Rāja Mān Singh of Gwalior, one of the greatest of Akbar's ministers, was also a great patron of music and is said to have introduced the dhrupad style of singing. The Gwalior court has maintained its high musical traditions to the present day.

The disciples of Tān Sen divided themselves into two groups, the *Rabābiyars* and the *Bīnkārs*. The former used the new instrument invented by Tān Sen, the *rabāb*; while the latter used the *bīn*, as the *vīṇā* is called in the north. Two descendants of these are living to-day at Rāmpur, a small state which has been famous for many centuries for its excellent musicians. The representative of the Bīnkārs is Muhammad Wazir Khān, whose paternal ancestor was Nabi Khān Bīnkār at the court of the Emperor, Muhammad Shah; and Muhammad Ali Khān is the representative of the Rabābiyars.

The heroic Mīrābāī (c. 1500), wife of a prince of the Udaipur clan and famous poetess and musician, and Tulsī Dās (1584), the singer and composer of the Hindī Rāmāyaṇa, are representatives of musical culture in North India.

Puṇḍarīka Viṭṭhal was probably another musician of Akbar's reign. He lived at Burhānpur in Khāndhesh and may have been asked to go over to Delhi when Akbar took Khāndhesh in 1599. Puṇḍarīka wrote four works:

Snaḍrāgachandrodaya, *Rāgamālā*, *Rāgamañjarī*, and *Nartananirṇaya* : these have recently been discovered in the State Library of Bikanir. It appears that the music of Upper India was getting into confusion, and Puṇḍarīka seems to have been asked by the Raja Burhānkhān to bring things into order. Puṇḍarīka was a southern paṇḍit, as he himself states, calling himself 'Karṇāṭika', or belonging to the south ; and so he had come to know both the northern and southern systems. He adopts the *śuddha* scale of the south and describes many northern *rāgas*. In describing his *rāgas* he seems to make use of only fourteen *śrutis* in the octave, and uses only twelve frets for his *vīṇā*.

Rāma Amātya, a southern musician, gives us the first detailed exposition of the southern system in the *Svaramela Kalānidhi*, written about the year A.D. 1550. This work contains the first collection of Indian *rāgas* which are adequately described. All of them belong to the Carnatic system and have shaḍja as their tonic. It seems that, in the south at least, *rāgas* have now been worked out from a common tonic, indicating that instrumental music had greatly developed.

Following this comes the *Rāgavibodha*, one of the most important works on Indian music, written in A.D. 1609 by Somanātha, a Telugu Brahman of the East coast, probably of Rajamandry. He was evidently a practical musician as well as a scholar and poet. The book is written in masterly couplets in the Ārya metre. It starts with the theory of musical sounds and goes on to describe the different *vīṇās* in existence and how to use them. The names and positions of the twenty-two *śrutis* are given. Somanātha belongs to the southern school and classifies the *rāgas* into primary and derivative (Janaka and Janya) as is done in modern south Indian music. He also gives a number of melodies developed from the *rāgas*. A translation of this work was appearing in the *Indian Music Journal* when it met with an untimely death.

Another important work of the southern school which was written about the same time is the *Chaturdaṇḍī Prakāśikā*, whose author was Paṇḍit Veṅkaṭamakhi, son of Govinda Dīkshit and pupil of Tānappāchārya, who is said to carry his *guruparamparā* (scholastic succession) right back to Śārṅgadeva himself. This work gives the basis of the present-day southern system and also of its *rāga* classification. The *rāgas* are arranged under seventy-two primary *rāgas*, called *Melakartas*, with a large number of derivative *rāgas* attached to each. This author makes use of the twelve semitones only in describing the *rāgas*.

In the northern school *Saṅgīta Darpaṇa*, or 'the mirror of music,' is a popular work written by Dāmodara Miśra about A.D. 1625, when Jahāngīr was Emperor. This book has become as unintelligible as the *Saṅgīta Ratnākara*, from which the author has freely copied most of his materials for the chapter on svaras. He has added a chapter on *rāgas* which is copied from some unknown author. Various pictorial descriptions of the different *rāgas* are given.

There were many good musicians at the court of Shāh Jahān (1628–66), among them being Jagannātha, who received the title Kavirāja; and Lāl Khān who was a descendant of Tān Sen. We are told that on one occasion Jagannātha and another musician named Dīraṅg Khān received from the Emperor their weight in silver, which amounted to about Rs. 4,500.

During the reign of Aurangzeb music went out of favour in the royal court. A story is told of how the court musicians, desiring to draw the Emperor's attention to their distressful condition came past his balcony carrying a gaily dressed corpse upon a bier and chanting mournful funeral songs. Upon the Emperor enquiring what the matter was, they told him that music had died from neglect and that they were taking its corpse to the burial ground. He replied at once, 'Very well, make the grave deep, so that neither voice nor echo may issue from it.'

The *Saṅgīta Pārijāta*, one of the most important works of the northern school, was written by Ahobala Paṇḍit in the seventeenth century. It was translated into Persian in the year 1724. Ahobala seems to have had access to both the *Rāgataraginī* and the *Rāgavibodha*. The *śuddha* scale of the *Pārijāta* is the same as that of the *Taranginī*. Ahobala recognizes twenty-nine *śrutis* altogether in the octave, but he rarely uses more than twelve to describe his *rāgas*. He gives altogether 122 different *rāgas*. The *Pārijāta* is the first work to describe the twelve *svaras* in terms of the length of the string of the *vīṇā*, so that we are able to reproduce to-day the notes that he used.

The next author of importance is Bhavabhaṭṭa, who was attached to the court of a rāja named Anupasiṅha. His ancestors came from the province of Ābhīra in Mālwā and his father was Janārdanabhaṭṭa, a musician at the court of Shāh Jahān. It is possible that he was the great musician of that name who obtained the title 'Kavirāja' from the Shāh. The family may have belonged to a southern stock, as he shows considerable acquaintance with the southern system of music. He classifies all the *rāgas* under twenty *thāṭs* (primary *rāgas*) and his *śuddha* scale is *Kanakāngī*, the *śuddha* scale of the south. He seems to have attempted to arrange the northern *rāgas* according to the southern system.

About this time Purandara Viṭṭhala wrote many beautiful songs in Kanarese, which are used to-day by the pupil as exercises at the beginning of his musical studies.

According to Sir S. M. Tagore, Muhammad Shāh (1719) was the last Emperor to have famous musicians at his court. Among them were Ādarāṅga and Sādarāṅga, two great Bīṅkārs. During this period the singer Shori perfected the Tappā style of Hindusthani singing. New types of song and music were also introduced, many of which were pleasing combinations of the Hindu and Persian styles.

In the early British period Indian music was generally confined to the courts of the leading Indian princes, as most Europeans regarded it as primitive and unscientific. There were, however, scholars like Sir William Jones and Sir W. Ousley and amateurs like Captain Day and Captain Willard who made a considerable study of it.

In South India, the Marāṭhā king of Tanjore, Tulajājī (A.D. 1763–1787) encouraged musicians by gifts and grants of land, so that they came to his court from the whole of India, and Tanjore became one of the most important musical centres in India. This king was also the author of an important treatise entitled *Saṅgīta Sārāmṛitam*.

The *Nāgmat-e-Asaphi*, written in A.D. 1813 by Muhammad Rezza, a nobleman of Patna, is a critical work on northern music. He pronounces the various northern systems of classification to be out of date and has no use for the *rāga-rāgiṇī-putra* basis upon which they build. He gives a new system of his own which brings together into groups *rāgas* which have similar features. This work is the first authority to take the Bilāval scale (similar to the European major mode) as its *śuddha* scale. This is the *śuddha* scale of the north to-day. The author tells us that he wrote the book after consulting the best artists available in his day. It is said that his *rāga lakshaṇas* (definitions) are still of use for Hindusthani musicians.

About this time Mahārāja Pratāp Singh of Jaipur (A.D. 1779-1804) called together a conference of musical experts and artists in Jaipur in order to arrange for a standard work on Hindusthani music. The book which resulted was called *Saṅgīta Sāra* or 'Epitome of Music.' The literary talent available does not seem to have been of a very high order, but it preserves for future reference the opinions of a body of musicians upon current thought and practice. Here also the *śuddha* scale is Bilāval, which by then seems to have been recognized as the regular Hindusthani *śuddha* scale.

Saṅgīta Rāgakalpadruma written by Kṛishṇānanda Vyāsa and published in Calcutta in 1842 collects together all the masterpieces then available of Hindī composition.

It should be remembered that all these authors use some form or other of the Sanskrit sol-fa notation which is the basis of the notation adopted in this book. (See Introduction).

While the northern system was thus trying to find a new basis of classification, the south was going ahead in musical composition. Tanjore was for many years one of the most important musical centres of India. It was here that

Tyāgāyya or Tyāgarāja, the great singer and poet (c. 1800–1850) composed and sang his songs, and gathered around himself a band of disciples who have continued his tradition till the present day. His charming *kṛitis* and *kīrtanas* are still sung all over the south. He was a creative musical genius and his compositions mark a definite advance in south Indian musical development. One who remembers him describes him as 'a tall lean man with a brown complexion.' He was revered as a perfectly sincere and selfless man. His father was Rāma Brāhman, who was also a musical composer of some repute. The *ṛishi* Nārada is said to have appeared to Tyāgarāja and to have presented him with a rare musical treatise entitled *Svarārṇava*. His teacher was Sunthi Veṅkaṭarāman. Music and religion were woven together in his life, and his songs were the outpourings of a real devotion. They were said to have been composed on *Ekādaśī* days, when he fasted all day long. Tyāgarāja introduced Saṅgatis—peculiar variations upon a particular melody—into his music. Each variation, while retaining the important features of the original melody, becomes more and more elaborate. Originality was the distinguishing mark of all his compositions.

Govinda Mārar was another well-known southern musician of this period. He lived in Travancore, a native state with a long and honourable musical tradition. Govinda Mārar was known as Shaṭkāla Govinda, because he could sing a piece in sextuple time. A story is related of his meeting with Tyāgarāja. A number of musicians including himself were seated with the master when a *pallavi* (chorus) in the *rāga pantuvarālī* was sung round by all. Govinda, using his own peculiar *tambūr* which had seven strings, sang it in shaṭkāla (sextuple) accelerated time. Tyāgarāja was so astonished that he gave him the name of Govindaswāmī and composed a song in his honour which began, 'There are many great men in the world and I respect them all.'

Muttuswāmī Dīkshita and Śyāma Śāstri were both contemporaries of Tyāgarāja. The former belonged to the Tinnevelly District and invented a new system of Indian notation which makes use of the different vowel syllables to indicate the various *vikṛits* of each *svara*. Ettiyāpuram Subrāma Dīkshita, his great grandson, has also written in Telugu a very important work on the southern system, which endeavours to apply the principles of Śārṅgadeva to modern music.

Many of the rājahs and princes of Cochin and Travancore were good musicians, among whom the most brilliant was Perumāl Mahārāja, whose compositions are in six languages: Sanskrit, Tamil, Telugu, Malayālam, Hindusthani, Marāṭhī.

In Bengal, in the latter half of the nineteenth century, Sir S. M. Tagore produced a number of important works on music. His *Universal History of Music* is a work of considerable value. The Bengal paṇḍits, including Tagore, adopted the old Hindusthani *rāga-rāgiṇī-putra* classification for their *rāgas.*

Dr. Rabindranath Tagore is a relative of Sir S. M. Tagore and exercises the most potent influence to-day upon music in Bengal. He has left the beaten tracks of Bengālī music and has made new paths for his melodies. His songs have rare musical and poetical qualities and are known all over Bengal.

The Indian rājahs and princes still have in their service many famous musicians, but unfortunately many of them depend almost entirely upon tradition in the rendering of *rāgas* and melodies. There seems to be no generally accepted system for Hindusthani music, though efforts are being made to-day by many scholars to work one out. The southern system, as readers will have guessed, is far more carefully systematized, and perhaps errs on the side of rigidity.

During the last few decades the scientific study of music in India has made great advances. Musical schools and associations have sprung up all over India; and to-day we find them in existence in such widely separated places as Bombay, Poona, Bangalore, Lahore, Gwalior, Baroda, Tanjore, Mysore, Trivandrum, Calcutta. The Gāndharva Mahā Vidyālaya, as the Bombay school is called, was first established in Lahore by Paṇḍit Vishṇu Digambar Paluskar in 1901 and then in Bombay in 1908. It has its nne head-quarters in Sandhurst Road and is supported by Mahārājas and government officials. The staff consists of forty teachers, both men and women, twenty-nine of whom belong to the Bombay branch; and its income is about Rs. 30,000 a year. Both vocal and instrumental music are taught, either individually or in classes. The school in Calcutta, under the name of Saṅgīt Saṅgha is a recent institution, and experiments are being made along the lines of the combination of the Indian and European systems.

The most noteworthy recent development has been the series of All-India Conferences, inaugurated in the year 1916 by His Highness the Mahārāja of Baroda, which led to the establishment of an All-India Music Academy in the year 1919. The Conference has been held annually since 1918, and has done a great deal of useful work in stimulating interest in and promoting the study of Indian music and in the systematization of Hindusthani *rāgas*. It has made possible the discussion of musical problems by a gathering of artists and experts drawn from the whole of India, a free interchange of thought and opinion by musicians of all races and climes in India, the attempt to find an adequate notation to express the beauties and refinements of Indian *rāgas* and melodies, and finally the establishment of this All-India Academy. The Academy is under the patronage of many of the leading Indian princes and has the support of men like Mr. N. V. Bhatkhande, who are giving themselves to the development of Indian music. It aims at providing facilities for collective and individual research, and for the collecting and preserving of the best classical compositions, and hopes to bring about a uniform method of arranging the *rāgas* and systematizing the melodies for the whole of India. The Academy of Music hopes, in co-operation with its sister organizations, to promote the development of a living musical culture, having its roots in the soil of India and expressing itself in nobler and more beautiful forms, so as to enrich the lives of both rich and poor.

CHAPTER III

THE DEVELOPMENT OF THE SCALE

The history of the Indian scale is really a series of close inferences; for the materials do not exist for definite and incontrovertible conclusions. This chapter aims at giving a general view of the development of the scale, based on scattered data gathered together in a fairly extensive reading of the various works which have appeared in India and elsewhere on the subject. It is not always possible to give references or to adduce the evidence for the conclusions arrived at, but the more curious reader should turn to one of the books mentioned in the Bibliography.

The principal data available for this study consist of brief references in ancient Indian literature, the tradition of the Sāman chant, the theory of the Grāma scales and the musical facts implied in the various *rāgas* used in the past or current to-day.

The scale of the Aryan peoples is based on the tetrachord (*chatuḥsvara*). The tetrachord is the fourth with its intervening notes. This may give the following tetrachords in the Indian scale: **SRGM, SrGM, SrgM**, and so on.[1]

The process whereby the tetrachord was first produced depends upon certain universal musical facts. The musical ear in search of a note does two things. It creeps up or down, one step at a time; and it makes a bold plunge for the nearest consonant note (*saṁvādī*) from the note which has been sounded (*vādī*). The voice has a tendency to ascend by leaps and to descend by steps. Music recognizes the following consonant intervals: the third, the

[1] See table on p. 5 for explanation.

fourth, the fifth, and the octave. In making a leap to the next consonant note, the choice really lies between the third and the fourth, as the fifth is too far away. The fourth is the more audible and many nations have chosen this in preference to the third. The fourth then becomes the upward limit of the tetrachord. When it comes to creeping up or down by what may be called 'next-door' notes, the chosen interval may be one of many or quite undefined. Most commonly the major tone or the semitone were the intervals chosen, though intervals of less than a semitone were also taken in India, as we shall see from the Sāman chant and from such a *rāga* as *Toḍī* (northern).

Consonance is called *Saṁvāditva* in India. Bharata divides *svaras* into four kinds, and this has remained the accepted division ever since. First there is the *vādī*, or sounding note, or sonant. Then the *saṁvādī*, the note consonant with the *vādī*. *Svaras* between which there is an interval of nine or thirteen *śrutis* are *saṁvādī* with each other. *Svaras* at an interval of two *śrutis* from the *vādī* are called *vivādī*, or 'dissonant' in relation to it. The others are called *anuvādī*, or 'assonant', i.e. neutral in relation to the *vādī*.

The *śruti* or microtonal interval is a division of the semitone, but not necessarily an equal division. This division of the semitone is found also in ancient Greek music. It is an interesting fact that we find in Greek music the counterpart of many things in Indian music, and we have a good deal of information about the development of Greek music; so we may look to get help from that source in our study of Indian music. The ancient Greek scale divided the octave into twenty-four small intervals, while the traditional Indian practice is to recognize twenty-two in the octave. Rao Sahib Abraham Paṇḍita, a south Indian musical scholar who has made a very close study of ancient Dravidian music, believes that the ancient Tamil books of the second and third century of our era support the view that in South India the octave was also divided into twenty-four equal intervals. Further investigation is being carried out in this matter, though, as has been already mentioned, a Tamil lexicon of the third or fourth century only gives twenty-two *mātras* for the octave, i.e. twenty-two *śrutis.* The *śruti* is really a kind of half-way house to the semitone. More than two *śrutis* are not usually sung in succession, though there are of course people who will sing the whole twenty-two of them in succession. Still that is acoustics and not music. So also the tetrachord might theoretically consist of as many notes as there are *śrutis* within the fourth, but practically it is difficult to sing or play more than four notes.

The Sāman chant is the earliest example of the Indian tetrachord which has remained until our time. In this the tetrachord is conceived of as a downward series of notes from the highest. Most of the early Indian modes, called Mūrchhanās, were also conceived as extending downwards. The Greeks too thought of the tetrachord in the same way.

The Sāman chant pivoted on two notes called the *udātta*—'raised'—the higher one, and the *anudātta*—'not raised', the lower one. In course of time the interval between these was established as a fourth. Then, later, the notes of this tetrachord received distinct names. The highest was *prathama*—'first'—then *dvitīya, tritīya, chaturtha,* down the scale. These names are found first in the *Ṛikprātiśākhya* (c. 400 B. C.). Later, a note called *svarita* is also mentioned, and this seems to be a graced *udātta,* thus indicating a note higher than the *prathama.* Later still we find this note definitely established and called *krushṭa*—'high' (*Taittirīya-prātiśākhya* c. A.D. 400). About the same time two other notes lower than the *chaturtha* appear. These are called *mandra*—'low', and *atisvārya*—'extremity'. This last was an extra note and was usually sung only in the cadence of the Sāman chant. So we find the whole series of the seven notes, or *svaras* as they were called, of the octave.

We must, however, remember that there is a South Indian tradition that the *rāga Ābhōgī* (**S R g M D**) represents the ancient Sāman chant. This is pentatonic, and there can be little doubt that the Sāman scale was pentatonic before it became heptatonic. We find that the pentatonic was the more primitive scale among all peoples.

It is the custom of Sāman singers to-day to call the higher tetrachord *uchcha*—'high', and the lower *nīcha* 'low'; but it seems probable that, while these terms may have originally only referred to a difference of position, later they came to mean a different style of singing. Sāman singers to-day seem to sing chromatically in the *uchcha* notes and diatonically in the *nīcha* notes.

'The voice is prior to the instrument. This is *prima facie* so probable that it can hardly be said to need proof. It is implied in the statement of Aristoxenus, that the natural laws of harmony cannot be deduced from instruments.' At any rate it is true that songs precede scales. It is impossible to think that a mother waited to sing a lullaby until a scale had been worked out in which to sing it. When people sing simple songs, they often know nothing about the intervals used in them, but they sing them all the same. We cannot say how people began to find them out. In out-of-the-way places singers use very few notes. Children use fewer than adults, country people fewer than townspeople, and flat-land dwellers fewer than mountaineers. It was a long time before the fifth was used and longer still before the octave came into use. The songs of primitive people were made up of a few musical intervals. Then as instruments were joined to the voice, they got accustomed to the third, the minor tone and the semitone. Then they began to sing diatonic series such as **S R G M,** or **S r G M,** and so on. Or they might proceed by a leap of two semitones, and then make the fourth, as in **S r g M**; or else the leap might come after the first semitone, as in **S r G M**. Then they might find a third way by using intervals of less than a semitone, as in **S r g M**. So the interval of the fourth became filled up partly by experiment and partly by theory.

The typical ancient Indian instruments were the drum (*dundubhi*), the flute (*muralī*), and the *vīṇā*. The *vīṇā* was used mainly in accompaniment, and the flute by itself, as when Krishṇa charmed the gopīs of Brindāban. As all music was largely improvization, the accompaniment could not be a strict following of the singer, though it is wonderful to see the way singer and player will keep close to one another all the time, even though neither has any piece of written music before him. Then also the instrument helped to register the notes and to define them. It was through the instrument that the importance of the major third, which has been called the *Magna Carta* of music, was realized. Further, through the instrument, the musician began to base his melody on the lower notes, as they are the louder and clearer on the instrument; whereas, when there was no instrument, he started from the higher notes and came downwards. It was also noted that the third obtained from the voice is slightly sharper than the third obtained from an instrument, eight *śrutis* as against seven *śrutis*. Bharata calls this difference of one *śruti* a *pramāṇa śruti*,—'indicative interval', because all the other intervals can be deduced from it, a fact which the Greeks also noted. So by the co-operation of voice and instrument the scale is worked out; and in one sense the instrument may be called 'the originator of the scale,' because it determines it.

It must, however, be remembered that a song or piece played on an instrument is a live thing and does not submit to mathematical precision. There is, it is true, only one form for each scale, and every singer and musician tries to get it right, though no one invariably manages to do so. The verv fact of putting passion (*rasa*) into music means that a particular note will be taken rather sharper at one time than at another. The law is there of course to be obeyed as perfectly as possible. In South India the use of the term *śruti* for such a possible sharpening or flattening of particular notes recognizes the truth of this variability. Music after all is an art and not a mere mechanism. Nobody can sing like a machine, even if he tries, any more than a man can walk in a perfectly straight line or breathe as the clock ticks.

The correlation of the notes of the Sāman chant with the notes of the secular or instrumental scale is another step in the process of this interrelationship of voice and instrument. We find evidence of this correlation as early as the *Ṛikprātiśākhya* in the statement that 'the *yama* (liturgical scale) is the *svara* (instrumental).' As we have seen, the Sāman scale was conceived as a downward series and the instrumental scale as an upward series. The names used for the instrumental scale in the ancient books are those in use to-day all over India. The clue to the interrelation of the two scales is found in the identification of *prathama* and *gāndhāra*. With this we get the two scales as follows, each forming a *saptaka* or 'cluster of seven.'

Sāman.		Secular.
		Nishādha
		Dhaivata
		Pañchama
Krushṭa	... ...	Madhyama
Prathama	... ...	Gāndhāra
Dvitīya	... ...	Ṛishabha
Tritīya	... ...	Shaḍja
Chaturtha	... ...	(Nishādha)
Mandra	... ...	(Dhaivata)
Atisvārya	... ...	(Pañchama)

The external relations of India in the early centuries of the Christian era are too obscure at present for us to be able to say whether the musical systems of Greece, Arabia and Persia have any definite relationship with that of India. It is certain that there was considerable intercommunication and commercial intercourse between India and each of these countries; and recent researches have shown the extent of Persian influence in India during the Maurya Empire (c. 300 B.C.) The musical systems of these countries show so much resemblance in certain essential features that it seems clear there must have been some connexion between them. The likeness is much closer than it is with the music of Japan or China. It is well known that Gāndhāra (the district of Kandahār) was in those early days a centre of Greco-Indian culture, as the Gāndhāran sculptures testify, and Taxila (near Rawalpindi) was the seat of a very important Buddhist university. Though Buddhism has never been associated with a special development of musical culture, the fact that a scale of considerable importance in those days was called Gāndhāra, and that one of the important notes of the gamut is known as Gāndhāra is of some significance. The two earliest Greek scales the *Mixolydic* and the *Doric*, show affinity with early Indian scales. All these things point to an interchange of ideas between the musical people of the two countries.

We have now come to see how the *gamut* of seven notes within the octave, including some smaller divisions, came to be accepted. These seven are called the *saptaka*, or 'cluster of seven,' and are known as the seven *svaras*. The first exposition of these various intervals is found in a Tamil work, *Tivākaram* (C. A.D. 200–300) of which mention has already been made. The scale was divided into twenty-two *mātras*, which are similar to the *śrutis* of the northern paṇḍits. The Tamil books also give them the name *alaku*. According to this work these twenty-two *śrutis* were distributed as follows :

Sa	**Ri**	**Ga**	**Ma**	**Pa**	**Dha**	**Ni**	
4	4	3	2	4	3	2	= 22

It is also rather interesting to find that the different intervals are described in relation to one another. **Sa** to **Ga** is recognized as a third, **Sa** to **Ma** as a fourth, **Sa** to **Pa** as a fifth, and **Sa** to **Dha** as a sixth : the fourth being called a 'friendly' interval, the fifth a 'related' interval, and the third and sixth 'enemy intervals.' The *Nāṭya Śāstra* (c. A.D. 500) shows a clear perception of the various intervals : octave, fifth, fourth, tone, minor tone and semi-tone. Each of these intervals is reckoned as having a certain number of *śrutis* as follows :—

Octave ...	... 22	*śrutis*	i.e.	1200 cents.
Fifth ...	... 13	,,	,,	702 ,,
Fourth ...	... 9	,,	,,	498 ,,
Tone ...	... 4	,,	,,	204 ,,
Minor Tone	... 3	,,	,,	182 ,,
Semi-tone...	... 2	,,	,,	112 ,,

The *śruti* numbers are really only approximations but the cents are of course accurate.

Thus the Indian scale divides the octave into twenty-two *śrutis*. As we have seen, the Greeks divided it into twenty-four small intervals. The three scales were as follows :—

Ni	Sa	Ri	Ga	Ma	Pa	Dha	Ni	
2	4	4	3	2	4	3		= 22 Indian (Tamil).
2	4	3	2	4	4	3		= 22 Indian (Bharata).
2	4	4	2	4	4	4		= 24 Greek.

The Indian became later

2	4	3	2	4	3	4

The Greeks seem to have made the change in the third interval from 2, 4, 4 to 2, 4, 3 in the early centuries of our era. The probable reason for this confusion is that these *śruti* numbers are more or less approximate to the actual vibration numbers. Thus the first three intervals may be either,

90	204	204	—	498	or,
112	204	182	=	498	

Neither the Greeks nor the Hindus in those days had any means of getting at the actual numbers, so that the *śruti* numbers in both countries may cover considerable variations.

The seven *svaras* of the *saptaka* current to-day throughout the whole of India are in the order of ascent from the note which has now become the Indian tonic: Shaḍja, Ṛishabha, Gāndhāra, Madhyama, Pañchama, Dhaivata, Nishādha. Their sol-fa initials, also current in every vernacular in India, are **Sa, Ri, Ga, Ma, Pa, Dha, Ni.** It is rather an interesting thing that the ancient Tamil names were quite different, viz. *Kural, Tuttam, Kaikkilai, Uḷai, Ili, Vilari, Tāram.*

As far as one can gather, the following are the root meanings of these Tamil names: *kural*, open tone; *kaikkilai*, unreciprocated passion; *uḷai*, place, side; *ili*, contempt, abuse; *vilari*, tenderness, compassion; *tāram* (Sanskrit) high.

It is clear that the Sanskrit names current now belong to some later period after the development sketched had taken place. Thus *shaḍja* means 'born of six' and indicates that this note which has now become the tonic was the last to arise in a downward series. *Madhyama* means 'middle' and suggests that when, at a much earlier period, this name was given, that note was the central note of the scale. The note *Gāndhāra* may be so called because it was the starting point of the Gāndhāra scale. *Pañchama* means 'fifth', i.e. from **Sa**, and implies a time when **Sa** had become the starting point of the scale. The other names do not imply any clear origin.

Hindu musical mythology refers each note to the tone of some animal. The cry of an animal tends to be always on the same note; and these names were intended no doubt to indicate in the first instance absolute pitch, and were later transferred to relative pitches. *Shaḍja* is said to be the sound produced by the peacock at its highest rapture. *Ṛishabha* is said to represent the sound made by the cow in calling her calf. *Gāndhāra* is the bleat of the goat. *Madhyama* is the cry of the heron. It is also called the tonic of nature, being identified with the sound of falling water, the roar of the forest and the buzz of great cities. *Pañchama* is the note of the kōkilā or Indian nightingale. *Dhaivata* is the neigh of the horse, and *Nishādha* the trumpeting of the elephant: the latter indicating clearly the lower note **Ni**, which was originally the starting point of the scale. Lower *Nishādha* is the first note of the Sāman scale, and so the elephant has been called *Sāmaja* or 'born of the Sāman.'

The next matter to which we have to devote attention is the history of the *grāmas*, or ancient scales. The first references to these are found in the *Mahābhārata* (A.D. 200) and the *Harivaṁśa* (A.D. 400). The former speaks of the 'sweet note Gāndhāra', probably referring to the scale of that name, since it is hardly likely that a single note would be called sweet. The *Harivaṁśa* speaks enthusiastically of music 'in the *grāmarāga* which goes down to Gāndhāra', and of 'the women of Bhīma's race who performed, in the Gāndhāra *grāmarāga*, the descent of the Ganges, so as to delight mind and ear.' In these two references the term used is *grāmarāga* and we may perhaps assume that it was the same as the Gāndhārī jāti of the *Nāṭya Śāstra*. The early Tamil works referring to music (*Tivākaram* and *Silappadigāram*) do not mention the grāmas. There is, however, something which seems to correspond to them, the *pālai*, of which there are four: formed, as are the derivative grāmas, by interchanging the *śruti* values of two notes.

Indian music is traditionally based on the three grāmas; and, though their history is involved in a confused mass of somewhat contradictory details through which one cannot always see light, it is necessary to try and understand the connection between them and the *rāgas* of to-day. The *Nāṭya Śāstra* gives particulars of two of these, the Sa-grāma and the Ma-grāma. (Adhy. 28 ślok. 41-45). The Ga-grāma is not mentioned until the *Ratnākara* (c. 1247). They are really fundamental scales starting from the notes **Sa**, **Ga**, and **Ma**, respectively. The formation of the Sa-grāma and the Ma-grāma is fairly clear.

The *śruti* values of the intervals of the Sa-grāma were as follows:—

Sa		**Ri**		**Ga**		**Ma**		**Pa**		**Dha**		**Ni**		**Sa**
	4		3		2		4		4		3		2	

The Ma-grāma is formed by interchanging the *śruti* values of the intervals before **Dha** and **Ni** and then starting on the **Ma**. Then it will be as follows:—

Ma		**Pa**		**Dha**		**Ni**		**Sa**		**Ri**		**Ga**		**Ma**
	4		3		4		2		4		3		2	

Thus the difference between this and the Sa-grāma lies in the sharpened fourth; the fourth in the first case consisting of nine *śrutis* and in the latter of eleven *śrutis*. This distinction has persisted until to-day, and we see it in one of the fundamental distinctions in the two main classes of *rāgas* both in the northern and the southern music, and particularly in the south, where it marks off one-half of the *rāgas*. The Ga-grāma is said by all the treatises to have been lost, and the directions given by the *Ratnākara* are not at all clear. Śārṅgadeva tells us to alter the frets of the vīnā in a certain way, but he does not tell us how the frets were placed before that alteration took place. If we take both the Sa-grāma and the Ma-grāma and do as Śārṅgadeva tells us, we come to an impossible scale. If, however, we take the theoretical Ma-grāma, i.e. the Ma-grāma with the *śruti* values changed as above, but still starting on the **Sa**, we come to something a little more reasonable. Then the Ma-grāma as suggested will be :—

Sa Ri Gạ Ma Pa Dha Ni Sa
4 3 2 4 3 4 2

This is the same as Bilāval, the fundamental scale of the north and also the present European major scale. Then obeying his directions, we get the result in *śruti* values :

2 4 4 3 2 4 3 (1)

This is the same as the Sa-grāma starting on **Ga**, thus : —

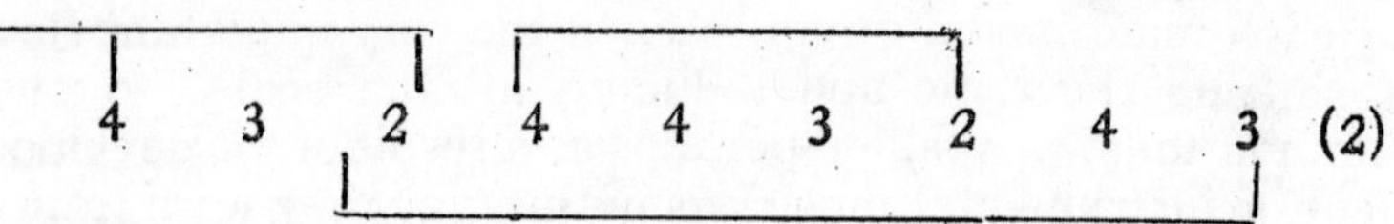

Why did he get at the Ga-grāma in this complicated way ? Being a musician he knew that the tonic of any scale needed the support of the drone strings, tuned to **Sa** and **Pa**. He got this by adopting (1) but he would not have got it by adopting (2) The following diagram shows how this was done :—

Sa Ri Ga Ma Pa Dha Ni Sa
Ma-grāma ... 4 3 2 4 3 4 2
New fretting ... 3 2 4 3 2 4 4
Sa Ri Ga Ma Pa Dha
New Sa-grāma 4 3 2 4 4 etc.
Ga-grāma | **Ga Ma Pa Dha**
2 4 4 3 etc.
Sa string | **Pa** string

The first note of his Ga-grāma is therefore in tune with his chief drone string, **Pa**. There is an established tradition that the Ga-grāma was abandoned because it was 'too high' for the voice. If, as we have seen, it was tuned a fifth higher than the Sa-grāma, the tradition may be explained : for a fifth is just the difference between two voice registers. It may also account for the statement that 'the Ga-grāma has gone to Indraloka (heaven)', being only fit for the heavenly singers' voices. This whole process is so complicated that it is no wonder that it went out of use. Śārṅgadeva himself only regarded it with antiquarian interest. The Ga-grāma is seen to-day in the *Bhairavī rāga*, (*Hanumatoḍī*) a typical minor *rāga*.

These grāmas were included in the local jātis, as they were called, being originally no doubt the different ways of singing practised in various parts of the country. These jātis were regarded as formations from either the Sa-grāma or the Ma-grāma, each starting on one note of the octave, thus forming seven jātis for each grāma. The early Tamil musical works also adopt the same method of forming fresh *pālai*, as they are called, there being seven for each main modal group. Then the very important step of shifting the tonic and reducing all the scales to one common tonic was taken, perhaps as a result of the development of instrumental music, as in this way they were transformed into simple instrumental scales. Perhaps the term *grāma rāga* which we have already come across, was first given to the jātis so reduced to the common tonic. This tonic, which may have been **Ni**, eventually became **Sa**, and then gradually the term *grāma* dropped out, as it had no real relation to actual facts, and they were called simply *rāgas*.

One of these *rāgas* is then regarded as the fundamental scale, or scale of *śuddha* or 'pure' notes; and all the other notes used in the other *rāgas* are thought of as *vikṛits* or 'variations.' It is interesting to find that the *śuddha* scale of the north is quite different from that of the south. In the north it is *Bilāval*, all the *vikṛits*, except that of Ma being flats of the *śuddha* notes. In the south it is *Mukhārī* (or *Kanakāṅgī*), in which all the *vikṛits* are sharps of the *śuddha* notes. Thus the former is what Europe calls a major scale, and the latter a minor scale. What is the explanation of these two *śuddha* scales, so different from each other? It may be that the southern *śuddha* scale—the minor one—is developed from the ancient Ga-grāma and the northern one from the ancient

Sa-grāma. It is very probable that the Ga-grāma was anterior to the Sa-grāma, though treatises make out the Sa-grāma to have been the original one. One is led to this idea because there is seen to be far closer correspondence between the Ga-grāma and the Sāman scale than between that and the Sa-grāma ; and also because, if the Ga-grāma was really developed from the other two, it is difficult to understand why it should have perished and the other two remained. Then, further, southern music sticks closer to the ancient model than northern music, which has been largely modified by contact with that of Persia and Arabia. In view of this suggestion it may be of interest to place down the *śruti* values of these two śuddha scales, so that they may be compared with the two grāmas.

Bilāval

Sa		Ri		Ga		Ma		Pa		Dha		Ni		Sa
	4		3		2		4		3		4		2	

Kanakāngī

Sa		Ri		Ga		Ma		Pa		Dha		Ni		Sa
	2		3		4		4		2		3		4	

It is easy to see how the latter could be developed from the Ga-grāma. The fourth of the Ga-grāma as given above has ten *śrutis*, which would naturally be reduced to nine so as to bring it into tune. Then the **Pa** must be kept in tune so as to be played on the open string of the vīṇā, and so it must be a fifth of thirteen *śrutis* from **Sa**. The other changes are very slight and do not alter the character of the scale. So it is possible that we see to-day the ancient grāmas in the two śuddha scales of India. Thus the scale in India is the result of a regular and scientific development of both vocal and instrumental music.

The scale as it exists to-day is one with great possibilities in regard to musical formations, and it has a very wide range in the microtonal variations included in it. The Indian musician is always trying to ornament his notes, because grace plays in the Indian system the part of harmony in the European. These ornaments are made by slight and indefinite variations, which may be quite different from what wo have called the *śrutis*, which are defined microtonal intervals used to bring notes into tune with one another. It may not be generally known that European singers and violin players aim at such definite microtonal differences under special circumstances, and whenever the accompanying harmonies do not preclude their doing so; but, unfortunately for them, these same harmonies have so limited their scope for indefinite *grace notes*, that their exuberance can find no better means for expressing itself than the *tremolo*; whereas, with no harmony to hamper his music, the Indian can reveal it in as many graces as he desires. The Indian scale, with all its *śrutis* and possibilities, resides in the bosom of the Indian musician, 'who is deąr to the gods'; and it only comes out in his songs, the intonation of which changes from day to day and from mood to mood.

CHAPTER IV

RĀGA—THE BASIS OF MELODY

Rāga is the basis of melody in Indian music and a substitute for the western scale. 'It is the attempt of an artistic nation to reduce to law and order the melodies that come and go on the lips of the people.' In *Rāga Vibodha*, it is defined as 'an arrangement of sounds, which possesses *varṇa*, furnishes gratification to the senses and is constituted by musical notes.' The term '*varṇa*' refers to the act of singing, and is of four kinds, viz.: *Sthāyī*-repetition of the same sound, *Ārohī*-ascent, *Avarohī*-descent, *Sañchārī*-ascent and descent mixed. Mr. Strangways defines *rāga* as 'an arbitrary series of notes characterized, as far as possible as individuals, by proximity to or remoteness from the note which marks the *tessitura* (general level of the melody), by a special order in which they are usually taken, by the frequency or the reverse with which they occur, by grace or the absence of it, and by relation to a tonic usually reinforced by a drone.' A simplified form of this might run: '*Rāgas* are different series of notes within the octave, which form the basis of all Indian melodies, and are differentiated from each other by the prominence of certain fixed notes and by the sequence of particular notes.' We may perhaps find in the term 'melody-type' the best way to transcribe *rāga* in English.

According to ancient musical theory, there are three important notes in the *rāga*. These are the Graha, the Aṁśa, and the Nyāsa. The Graha is the starting note. the Aṁśa the predominant, and the Nyāsa the ending note. The aṁśa is also called the vādī. Very little importance is attached to the graha and the nyāsa to-day, and it is quite possible that they were, in the *Ratnākara*, the technical terms for the terminal notes of the tetrachord and not of the *rāga*. The aṁśa, however, is all-important and is called the jīva or 'soul of the *rāga*.' The position of the aṁśa has much to do with the general character of the *rāga*. Occasionally it varies between two notes. The aṁśa is not so distinctly differentiated in the music of the south, and this may point to a further development there.

All the characteristics of the *rāga* are embodied in its Mūrchhanā or Thāṭ, which are the names now given in the south and the north respectively to the *rāga* basis expressed in notes. The aṁśa, and also the peculiar sequences and grace notes of the *rāga*, are shown in this, which includes both ascent and descent. It includes all the essential facts about the *rāga* which the musician should know before composing any melody in it.

Rāgas have probably originated from four main sources 1. Local tribal songs; 2. Poetical creations; 3. Devotional songs; 4. Compositions of scientific musicians. Many of these sources may be traced in their names. *Bhairavī* means 'an ascetic'; *Hindol* is 'a swing'; *Kānaḍā* refers to the Carnatic; *Multānī* means 'belonging to the city of Multān'; and *Megh* means 'the rainy season', and so on.

We can see the same processes of formation going on to-day. Dr. Rabindranath Tagore creates new melodies from the old folk songs of Bengal. Some one finds an old Portuguese melody and puts it into an Indian setting and calls it *Portuguese Tappā*, as it is modelled on the well-known Hindusthani *Tappā* form of melody. A famous musician takes an old *rāga* and introduces some unconventional variation, and the result becomes a new *rāga* named after him. Miyān Tān Sen, for example, introduced **Ga** and both varieties of **Ni** into the *rāga Mallār*, which omits them as a rule; and the result is the *rāga Miyān-ki-Mallār*. There are quite a number of varieties of the *rāga Mallār* by different musicians. Then others combined two or more *rāgas* into a new one. Amīr Khusru took Hindol and a Persian melody, Mokam, and formed *Yaman*. Another takes Sāraṅga, Sindhu and Mokam, and the result is a new *rāga Ushaq*. Or a northern musician comes across a good southern *rāga*, and introduces it in its southern for into the northern music, as Mr. Kirloskar, the Poo dramatist, did with the southern *rāgas Kāṁbodhi* a *Ārabhī*. Southern musicians do the same with the no thern *rāgas*, sometimes prefixing the term *Deśika* Hindusthan, as *Hindusthan Bihāg*, *Deśika Khamāj* an so on. This is a living process which we may watch to day all over India.

The question of the systematic classification of th *rāgas* presents considerable difficulty. For the last 35 years the south has had a more or less uniform system which has crystallized into the present form. Northern musicians, however, have had as many systems as musicians Bharata gives only fourteen melody-bases, which he call *Jātis* and *Mūrchhanās*, developed from either the Sa o the Ma-grāma. These were developed by shifting th tonic or starting note to each note of the scale, thu forming seven for each mode. This same practice has been followed in the early Tamil books. Then Śārṅgadeva enumerates 264 *rāgas* under the two grāmas. The *Rāgmālā* of Puṇḍarīka adopts the northern method of classifying *rāgas* into six principal *rāgas*, with wives, or secondary *rāgas*, and children, or derivative *rāgas*. The two latter are called *ragiṇī* and *putra*. A considerable number of new *rāgas* are added by him. The *Rāga Vibodha* adopts the southern system and recognizes twenty-three primary *rāgas* with a large number of secondary *rāgas*. The primary *rāgas* of this work are *Mukhārī* (*i.e. Kanakāṅgī*) *Revagupta*, *Sāmavarāḷī*, *Toḍī*, *Nādarāmakriyā*, *Bhaïrava*, *Vasanta*, *Vasanta-bhairava*, *Mālavagauḷa*, *Rītigauḷa*, *Abhīranāṭa*, *Hamīra*, *Śuddha-varāḷī*, *Śuddharāmakriyā*, *Śrī*, *Kalyāṇī*, *Kāṁbodhi*, *Mallār*, *Samātha*, *Karṇāṭagauḷa*, *Deśākshī*, *Śuddhanāṭa Sāraṅga*. Somanātha carefully describes each *rāga* and many of them are found in the same form to-day. The *Saṅgīta-Darpaṇa* builds up a most fanciful theory on the northern model, and this has nominally remained the principal theory of the north until to-day. Bhavabhaṭṭa attempts a rearrangement of the northern *rāgas* on a somewhat similar system to that of the south, adopting twenty primary *rāgas*. Then Muhammad Rezza suggested a new arrangement of the northern system on the principle that there should be some real affinity between the *rāga*, *rāgiṇī* and *putra*, a principle which seems self-evident, but which has not been really adopted by the north; for it is almost impossible to get from the northern musician a reasonable account of the basis of the present-day classification. Meanwhile, in the south, Veṅkaṭamakhi provided a sound system based on scientific principles which has continued to this day. The Carnatic system will be first described.

I. THE CARNATIC SYSTEM

All *rāgas* are first divided into two main classes, primary or *Janaka rāgas*, and secondary or *Janya rāgas*. The first class are also called the Melakartas or 'Lords of Melody'. They number seventy-two and are formed by variations of the seven notes of the gamut in regular order, ascending and descending. They are also known as the *Sampūrṇa rāgas*, as they contain all the notes of the gamut and are not transilient anywhere. These seventy-two are again divided into two classes by the use of the sharpened fourth (i.e. Tīvra or Prati Ma). The first thirty-six use the Śuddha Ma (regular fourth), and the last thirty-six the Prati Ma (sharpened fourth). We see in this the survival of the difference between the ancient Sa and Ma-grāmas.

The first *rāga* is the scale of śuddha notes and is called *Kanakāṅgī*. It is the ancient *Mukhārī* and runs as follows:

It is a most strange scale to western ears and is not common in south India to-day. Judging by the *Ratnākara* and the *Svaramela-Kalānidhi*, it was very popular in the sixteenth century. It corresponds with the ancient Greek chromatic scale.

The most common *rāga* in the south to-day is *Māyāmālavagauḷa*—the *Bhairava rāga* of the north.

This *rāga* is very popular, and most southern musicians begin to learn music with this. It has quite a pleasing sound, in spite, or perhaps, because of the intervals of three semi-tones between the second and third, and between the sixth and seventh. It has been suggested that the *rāga Māyāmālavagauḷa* may have developed from the *rāga Mukhārī* (*Kanakāṅgī*) by a modal shift of tonic one semitone higher, just as the modern Greek scale has done. Thus

Māyāmālavagauḷa (C to C)

B C D♭ E F G A♭ B C

Mukhārī (B to B)

B to B forms the *rāga Mukhārī* and C to C is *Māyāmālavagauḷa*.

The most important primary *rāgas* are found in the first thirty-six, with a few exceptions. The latter group of thirty-six correspond in every particular, except in the use of Prati Ma, with the *rāgas* of the first group, one by one. Each *rāga* starts now from the one tonic, shaḍja, thus giving rise to the idea that the grāmas have entirely disappeared; but it is still possible to see them surviving in many of the peculiarities of the *rāgas*.

Carnatic Primary Rāgas

N.B.—The Aṁśa note has a double line underneath.

The name in brackets is that of the corresponding northern *rāga*. The number at the side is that of the *rāga* in the regular southern scheme. There is also added the time when the *rāga* should be used and the passion or mood associated with it.

8. *Hanumatoḍī* (*Bhairavī*). Morning, sad.

15. *Māyāmālavagauḷa* (*Bhairava*). Dawn, reverence.

The Arabs have a mode similar to this called Hyāz.

16. *Chakravāham* (*Ānandabhairava*). Any time, love.

20. *Naṭabhairavī* (*Sindhubhairavī*). Night, sad.

This is the same as the Hypo-Dorian plagal mode.

22. *Kharaharapriyā* (*Kāphī*). Noon, passion.

This is the Dorian mode.

28. *Harikāmbodhi* (*Jhiñjhoṭī*) Night, imploring, aise.

This is the Hypo-Lydian plagal mode.

29. *Śaṅkarābharaṇa* (*Bilāval*). Morning, calm.

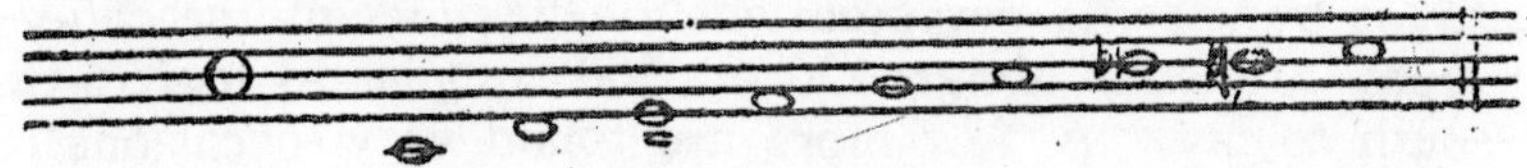

This is the western major mode, with a slight difference in the sixth.

36. *Chalanāṭa* (*None*). Night, boldness.

45. *Śubhapantuvarāḷī* (*Tōḍī*). Evening, adoration.

This probably arose from an ancient enharmonic scale basis.

53. *Gamanapriyā* (*Mārvā*). Evening, passion.

65. *Mechakalyāṇī* (*Kalyān*). Evening, merriment.

This is the Lydian authentic mode with the addition of F ♯

All the *rāgas* given above are primary *rāgas*, called *janaka rāgas* or *melakartas*. From these are formed the secondary or *janya rāgas*. Though it is theoretically possible to form a very large number of these secondary *rāgas* by varying combinations of the notes of the octave, there are only about 400 or 500 in general use in the south to-day. A few more are found very occasionally, but altogether the total of those used will not come to more than 800. The secondary *rāgas* are formed by combining in various ways five or more of the notes used in the primary *rāga* under which they are grouped. With the exception of a few *rāgas*, it is the rule to use in the secondary *rāga* only those *śrutis* which are used in the primary *rāga*. Musical experts look askance at the introduction of unauthorized accidentals.

The following are the ways in which these secondary *rāgas* are formed :—

1. By the omission of certain notes in the ascent or descent or in both, thus forming a transilient series. *Rāgas* which only use five notes in both ascent and descent are called *Oḍava rāgas*, i.e. Pentatonic. Those using six only are known as *Shāḍava*, i.e. Hexatonic. Among the *Oḍava rāgas* are found some of the most beautiful of Indian *rāgas* and some of the most widely used.

The following are a few of the most important of these transilient *rāgas* :—

(The name of the corresponding northern *rāga* is put in brackets).

Dhanyāsī. Primary, *Hanumatoḍī* (variety of *Bhairavī*).

This is a very charming and plaintive *rāga*, used especially in songs of pleading. Its characteristic phrase is **P n Ṡ** (G B♭ C). Its aṁśa is Ni. The omitted note Dha is often used as a grace note, when descending from the Sa, after the characteristic phrase.

Madhyamāvatī. Primary, *Kharaharapriyā.* (*Sāraṅga*) This is a very beautiful pentatonic *rāga*, used in songs of meditation. Its characteristic phrase is **R M n** (D F B♭) with both Ri and Ma as aṁśa notes.

Mohana. Primary, *Harikāmbodhi.* (*Bhūpālī*). A very common and popular *rāga*, used for joyful songs. It is strictly pentatonic. It is also the scale of the Scotch bagpipes, and is one of the primitive scales of both Arabia and China. The well-known hymn 'There is a happy land' is written in this *rāga*, and the tune seems to have come from South India. Its characteristic phrase is **G P D** (E G A) and its aṁśa note is Ga.

Ārabhī. Primary, *Śaṅkarābharaṇa.* (*Ārabhī*). A *rāga* fully pentatonic both in ascent and descent. It is frequently used in devotional songs. It was introduced to the north in its southern form and with the same name by the dramatist Kirloskar. Its special phrase is **R M D** (D F A) with the aṁśa on Ma.

Haṁsadhvani. Primary, *Śaṅkarābharaṇa.*

This fascinating pentatonic *rāga* is also used a great deal in devotional songs and in love songs too. Its characteristic phrase is **G P N** (E G B), with Pa as its aṁśa.

Śuddhanāṭa. Primary, *Chalanāṭa.*

This is a fully pentatonic *rāga*. It is a *rāga* of power and majesty and is popular with expert musicians. It has a most distinct and fascinating flavour. The leap phrase **S G M** (C E F) has a great deal to do with this. Its aṁśa is Ga.

Toḍī. Primary. *Hanumatoḍī.* (*Bhairavī*).

This is one of the most common of the southern *rāgas*. The Pa is omitted altogether in the ascent, but is often lightly touched in the descent. The leap from Ma to Dha and its minor tones make it a very attractive *rāga*. It is a *rāga* of majesty. The aṁśa is usually Dha, but is sometimes shifted to Ma. Its characteristic phrase is **g M d** (B♭ F A♭).

Devamanoharī. Primary, *Kharaharapriyā.* (*Sāraṅga*) This is a *Shāḍava rāga* with the Ga omitted in both ascent and descent. The descent, however, varies from the ascent. The phrase **S n D P n P** (C B♭ A B𝄳 G), with a slide from the Ni to the Pa, occurs frequently in the descent. Ri is its aṁśa.

Kāmbodhi. Primary, *Harikāmbodhi.* (*Khamāj* or *Jhinjhoṭī*). This *rāga* is hexatonic in the ascent only. Its peculiar phrase is **P D S̄ n** (G A D B♭), and it uses both varieties of Ni, the accidental being found specially in connection with the phrase **S̄ N P D S̄**. It is a very common *rāga* and is used in devotional songs of praise.

Hindolam. Primary, *Naṭabhairavī.* (*Mālkos*). This is quite different from the northern *Hindol* which, however, has the same swinging rythm. The northern *Hindol* comes in the *Gamanapriyā Mela* and so uses the sharpened fourth. This *rāga* is used for love songs of a joyful character. The swing phrases are easily noted. Its aṁśa is Ma.

2. The other way of forming the secondary *rāgas* from the primary is by peculiar combinations, making use of all the notes of the octave in varying order, in ascent or descent or in both. The following are some of the most important of these.

Punnāgavarāḷī. Primary, *Hanumatoḍī.*

This *rāga* usually starts on Ni and it has Sa for its aṁśa. It is specially used for songs of sorrow, and has a rather low tessitura. Its characteristic phrase is **S g M d** (C E𝄳 F A𝄳).

Nādanāmakriyā. Primary, *Māyāmālavagauḷa.* (*Kālangaḍā*). This is very popular, especially for religious folk songs and also for earnest songs of devotion. Its characteristic phrase is **S r M g M** (C D𝄳 F E F♯) and its aṁśa is Ma.

Ānandabhairavī. Primary, *Naṭabhairavī* (*Ānandabhairavī*). This is a morning *rāga* especially used for religious songs. It has two peculiar phrases, one in the first tètrachord and one in the second. The first is **S g R g** (C E𝄳 D E𝄳) and the second **P S̄ n d P** (G C B𝄳 A𝄳 G). The latter is a very beautiful leap phrase. In this *rāga* the Ni is often sharpened in the descent, so that it almost becomes Śuddha Ni, B♮ is used instead of B𝄳, and it also makes use of a sharpened Ga in the descent, which is practically Śuddha Ga (E♮). Its aṁśa is Ga.

Bilaharī. Primary, *Śaṅkarābharaṇa.*

A very sweet *rāga* associated with morning songs of joy. It may be sung up to noon. It is a south Indian *rāga* and is not found in the north. This *rāga* is very commonly used for wedding melodies. Captain Day notes one in his book which is still popular. It has two leaps, one from the third to the fifth and the other from the sixth to the octave, both in the ascent. Its characteristic phrase is **D Ṡ N D** (A C B A) and it has Pa as its aṁśa.

Hamīrkalyāṇī. Primary, *Mechakalyāṇī.* (*Hamīrkalyāṇī*). This *rāga* is one of those using the sharpened fourth. It belongs to the latter thirty-six. It uses the Śuddha Ma also sometimes. There are a number of *rāgas* which do the same. This *rāga* is one of the joyful wedding *rāgas* of India in both north and south.

Śrīrāga. Primary, *Kharaharapriyā.*

The northern Śrī is quite different, and belongs to the *Kāmavardhanī* or *Rāmapriyā* Mela, having the sharpened fourth. The southern Śrī is a most fascinating *rāga* with a flavour of haunting sadness, and is used in songs of sorrow. The ascent is pentatonic and there are three special phrases: **S R M P n** (C D F G B♭), **S R n S** (C D B♭ C), **P n D P n Ṡ** (G B A G B♭ C). Śuddha Ga is often used instead of komal Ga in the descent.

There are of course many other popular and beautiful *rāgas*, but space does not allow us to add any more here. It is an interesting fact that one of the most popular of the southern primary *rāgas* is *Śaṅkarābharaṇa*, which is the western major mode. This and the *Harikāmbodhi Mela* are the two most common primary modes in the south, judging from the number of secondary *rāgas* connected with them. This does not correspond with a very general opinion in western countries, that Indian music is all in the minor modes. Among the most popular *rāgas* in the *Śaṅkarābharaṇa Mela* are the sweet *Kānaḍā* with its pretty lilts; *Navaroj* always sung in the middle register; the sweet and plaintive *Nīlāmbari*; the bright and merry *Surānandinī*; the proud *Adāṇā* with its peculiar phrase **P D N D** (G A B A); *Bihāgaḍā*, the *rāga* of argument, using both śuddha Ni and komal Ni; the pleasant *Bihāg*, beloved both in north and south: the stately *Ḍarbārī*, and very many more. The next most popular melas are *Naṭabhairavī* and *Kharaharapriyā*, both of which are in the minor mode, having two flats each. These two *rāgas* and their secondaries are often used in religious songs.

Māyāmālavagauḷa and *Hanumatoḍī* are the only other primary *rāgas*, with a large number of secondary *rāgas* connected with them. Both of them have a characteristic flavour and are very popular. The former group supplies many of the melodies for the folk-songs of the people, sung by the bullock-cart driver, the boatman and the labourer.

One must emphasize the point that these *rāgas* are not the melodies themselves but the groundwork from which the melodies are afterwards formed. A thousand different melodies may be composed upon the same *rāga*.

Many of the *rāgas* have characteristic grace notes attached to them. In *Bihāg* Ri is only used as grace, and in *Bihāgaḍā* Ni is always played with the grace note Sa. In *Hamīrkalyāṇī* Ga has its grace note, and so on. These grace notes are essential constituents of the *rāga* and not simply accidentals as in western music.

Carnatic Secondary Rāgas

The characteristic phrase is shown at the right-hand side.

Dhanyāsī. Primary, *Hanumatoḍī*. (Variety of *Bhairavī*). Morning, pleading.

Bhūpāla. Primary, *Hanumatoḍī*. Early morning, praise.

Madhyamāvatī. Primary, *Kharaharapriyā.* (*Sāraṅga*). Noon, calm.

Mohana. Primary, *Harikāmbodhi.* (*Bhūpālī*). Noon, sweetness.

Ārabhī. Primary, *Śaṅkarābharaṇa.* (*Ārabhī*). Morning, mystery.

Haṁsadhvani. Primary, *Śaṅkarābharaṇa.* Noon, entreaty, expostulation.

Śuddhanāṭa. Primary, *Chalanāṭa.* Night, power and majesty.

Toḍī. Primary, *Hanumatoḍī.* (*Bhairavī*). Morning, sad.

S r g M d n Ṡ Ṡ n d P M g r S g M d

Devamanoharī. Primary, *Kharaharapriyā.* (Variety of *Sāraṅga*). Night.

S R M P D n Ṡ Ṡ n D n P M R S

Kāmbodhi. Primary, *Harikāmbodhi.* (*Khamāj* or *Jhinjhoṭī*). Evening and night, praise.

S R G M P D Ṡ Ṡ N n D P M G R S P D Ṡ n

Hindolam. Primary, *Naṭabhairavī.* (*Mālkos*). Evening, gay.

S M g M d n Ṡ Ṡ n d M g S

Punnāgavarāḷī. Primary, *Hanumatoḍī.* Night, melancholy.

ṇ S r g M P d n n d P M P g r S

Nādanāmakriyā. Primary, *Māyāmālavagauḷa.* (*Kālaṅgaḍā*). Evening, calm.

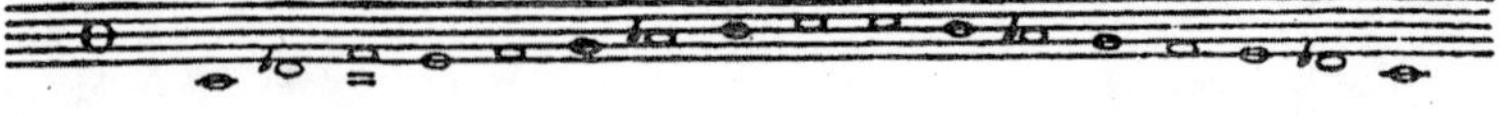

S r M G M P d N Ṡ Ṡ N d P M G r S

Ānandabhairavī. Primary, *Naṭabhairavī*. Morning, devotion.

Bilaharī. Primary, *Śaṅkarābharaṇa*. Morning, joy.

Hamīrkalyāṇī. Primary, *Mechakalyāṇī*. (*Hamīr-kalyāṇī*). Evening, merriment.

Śrīrāga. Primary, *Kharaharapriyā*. Evening, sadness.

II. Hindusthani Rāgas

The general remarks made in the section above on the Carnatic *rāgas* apply as a rule to the *rāgas* of the north also. The nomenclature is usually quite different, except in the cases of those *rāgas* which have been avowedly borrowed from the other system. Not only so, but it is not easy to attempt any description of the Hindusthani system, as most scholars have their own way of classifying the *rāgas*. The basis which is adopted by the majority of the northern musicians is known as the *Rāga-rāgiṇī-putra* basis. It is a somewhat fanciful system the details of which depend very largely upon the choice of each individual. There are supposed to be six principal *rāgas*, each one of which has a number of *rāgiṇīs*, or wives, attached to it, these two having a number of *putras*, or sons. There does not seem to be any definite qualities which determine the particular *rāgas* which must belong to each one of these groups, or which form the principle of attachment to a particular *rāga*. The result is that there are almost as many systems of classification as there are musicians. The tendency among scholars and practical musicians to-day is to put aside altogether this old system, and to adopt a more rational one based on somewhat similar lines to that of the southern system.

Many different lists of the six principal *rāgas* are given. Among them the following are the most important:—

Puṇḍarīka. Bhairava, Hindol, Deśakār, Śrī, Nāṭa, Naṭṭanārāyaṇa.

Muhammad Rezza. Bhairava, Mālakauṅśa, Hindol, Śrī, Megh, Nāṭa.

Rajah S. M. Tagore. Śrī, Vasanta, Bhairava, Pañchamā, Megh, Naṭṭanārāyaṇa.

Sir W. Jones. Bhairava, Mālava, Śrī, Hindol, Dīpak, Megh.

It will be noticed that every list contains the two names, Bhairava and Śrī. Bhairava is the Māyāmālavagauḷa of the south and Śrī is the Rāmapriyā rāga. Nearly all the other lists, with only a few exceptions, also contain these two names. Among the other names, Megh and Nārāyaṇa are varieties of Śaṅkarābharaṇa. Vasanta corresponds to Gamanapriyā, having the sharpened fourth, and Hindol is also a member of this mela. The name *thāṭ* is the northern term for *melakarta*, or primary *rāga*.

From time to time various scholars have tried to introduce system and order into the classification of the northern school. Bhavabhaṭṭa was one of the first to undertake this, and he proposed to select twenty main thāṭs as primary *rāgas*. They were: 1. Toḍī, 2. Gauḍa, 3. Varāṭī, 4. Kedāra, 5. Śuddhanāṭa, 6. Mālavakaiśikā, 7. Śrī, 8. Hamīr, 9. Āhirī, 10. Kalyāṇī, 11. Deśākshī, 12. Deśakār, 13. Sāraṅga, 14. Karṇāṭa, 15. Kāmoda, 16. Hijhāja, 17. Nādarāmakriyā, 18. Hindol, 19. Mukhārī, 20. Soma. No other musician, however, has adopted this basis.

In recent years Mr. N. V. Bhatkhande of Bombay has put forward a classification which seems to be based on reasonable principles, and is on the way to acceptance by a large number of musicians and scholars. The following are the general lines of his proposals:—

The names in brackets are those of corresponding southern *rāgas*.

I. *Bilāval group* (*Śaṅkarābharaṇa*).

Those having the first tetrachord of the western major mode, with Śuddha or Tīvra Dha in the second half.

S R G M P D or n N S

C D E F G A A♯ B C

Included in this group are the following:—

Bihāg, Kakubh, Deśakār, Durgā.

II. *Yaman or Kalyāṇī group* (*Kalyāṇī*).

Similar to the Bilāval group, with the exception of the substitution of Tīvra Ma for Śuddha Ma.

S R G m P D or n N S

C D E F♯ G A A♯ B C

Included under this group come:—

Hamīr, Kedāra, Kāmoda, Śyāma.

III. *Khamāj group* (*Harikāmbodhi*).

This is a modification of the Bilāval group by the change of Śuddha Ni to Komal Ni.

S R G M P D n S

C D E F G A B♭ C

The principal *rāgas* under this are:—

Jhinjhoṭī, Tilaṅga, Khambāvatī, Tilak-kāmoda, Jayajayavantī.

Some of these *rāgas* use both varieties of Ni.

IV. *Bhairava group* (*Māyāmālavagauḷa*).

This has the first tetrachord of Bhairava, with either Komal or Śuddha Dha, and either Komal or Śuddha Ni.

S r G M P d or D n or N S

C D♭ E F G A♭ A♮ B♭ B♮ C

The following are included in this group :—

Bhairava, Kālaṅgaḍā, Meghrañjanī, Saurāshṭī, Jogiyā, Rāmkalī, Bibhās, Ābherī-bhairava, Lalitā, Sāverī, Ānanda-bhairava, Guṇakrī, Hijhāja.

V. *Pūrvī group.* (*Kāmavardhanī*).

This is differentiated from the Bhairava group by the use of Ma Tīvra instead of Ma Śuddha.

S	r	G	m	P	d	N	S
C	D♭	E	F♯	G	A♭	B	C

The following are included under this group :—

Śrī, Jetāśrī, Ṭaṅkī, Pūriyā-dhanāśrī, Mālavī, Gaurī.

Śrī rāga is first mentioned by Hṛidaya Prakās (1667); and Hṛidaya Nārāyaṇa Dev, Rajah of Gadadeś, is said to be its originator.

VI. *Mārvā group.* (*Gamanapriyā*).

The difference between this and the preceding group is only in the use of Śuddha and Tīvra Dha for Komal Dha.

S	r	G	m	P	D	or	n	N	S
C	D♭	E	F♯	G	A		A♯	B	C

The following belong to this group :—

Hindol, Pūriyā, Pañchamā, Deśakār, Gaur-pañchamā.

VII. *Kāphī group.* (*Kharaharapriyā*).

These all have the first tetrachord of Kāphī, with Ni Komal in the second half.

S	R	g	M	P	D	n	S
C	D	E♭	F	G	A	B♭	C

The following are included in this :—

Pilu, Dhanāśrī, Vāgīśvarī, Sūhā, Bhīmpalāsī, Sāraṅga.

VIII. *Āsāvarī group.* (*Naṭabhairavī*).

This group only differs from the Kāphī group in the use of Dha Komal for Śuddha Dha.

S	R	g	M	P	d	n	S
C	D	E♭	F	G	A♭	B♭	C

The principal *rāgas* under this are :—

Gāndhārī, Jaunpurī, Deśī.

IX. *Bhairavī group.* (*Hanumatoḍī*).

This is another modification of the Kāphī group, formed by using Komal Ri and Komal Dha instead of the Śuddha varieties.

S r g M P d n Ṡ
C D♭ E♭ F G A♭ B♭ C

It may be noted that all the alterable notes here are Komal.

The secondary *rāgas* attached to it are Bhūpāla, Jaṅgalā, Mukhārī, Āsāvarī, Dhanāśrī, Mālkos. The latter is one of the most popular of north Indian *rāgas*.

X. *Toḍī group.* (*Śubhapantuvarāḷī*).

This is a mixed group formed by *rāgas* having the first tetrachord of Bhairavī and the second of Pūrvī and using in addition the sharpened fourth. It also makes use of a sharpened seventh, somewhat sharper than Śuddha Ni.

S r g m P d N or N^+ $\bar{S}$
C D♭ E♭ F♯ G A♭ B B♯ C

In this group microtonal variations are frequently used. The Ri will be Atikomal, and the Dha and Ma will be less than the full sharpened semitones. So that the true signature should be **S r^- g^- m P d^- N^+ S.** The principal *rāgas* connected with it are Gurjarī, Multānī.

It will be noted that Mr. Bhatkhande has chosen ten of the southern melakartas (primary *rāgas*) for his primary *rāgas*, and he then classifies all the other northern *rāgas* under these. As will be seen from the lists of *rāgas* which follow with their notation, some of them use variants under the groups. Each group reveals a distinct characteristic, and we can see the musical affinities which bring the *rāgas* in each group together. It is possible that this system may express the musical facts better even than the strictly logical system of the south.

It is possible further to subdivide each one of these groups by means of such factors as the following. Those which have no Ma in either ascent or descent; shāḍava *rāgas*; those having both Śuddha and Tīvra Ma, and so on. In this way a really useful classification of Hindusthani *rāgas* may be arrived at; and probably during the course of the next few years it will be worked out thoroughly so as to come into common use. Until some such scheme is accepted, it will be very difficult to find a common basis for the northern and southern musical systems. In a short account like this it is not possible to pursue further this classification of *rāgas.*

Hindusthani Rāgas

The name in brackets is the corresponding Carnatic rāga.

I. *Bilāval.* (*Śankarābharaṇa*). Western major mode. Morning, joy.

S R G M P D n- N Ṡ

Bihāg. Bilāval group. (*Bihāg*). Night, love, tenderness.

S G M m P N Ṡ Ṡ N D P M G R S

Durgā. Bilāval group. (*Śuddhasāverī*). Morning.

S R M P D Ṡ Ṡ D P M R S

II. *Yaman.* (*Mechakalyāṇī*). Evening, merriment.

S R G m P D N Ṡ

Kedāra. Yaman group. (*Kedāra*). Evening, gay.

S M m P D n N Ṡ Ṡ N D P m M G R S

Kāmoda. Yaman group. Evening.

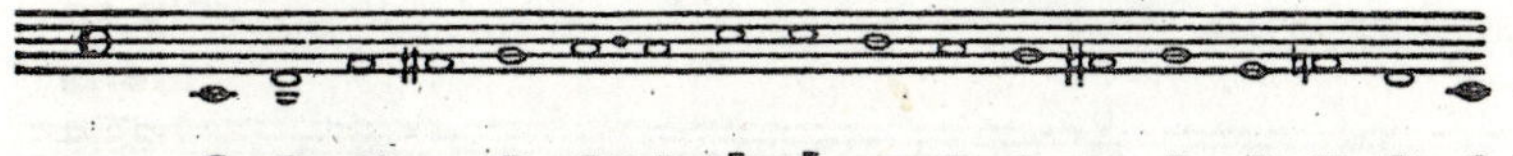

S R M m P D N D S̄ S̄ N D P m P G M R S

III. *Khamāj.* (*Harikāmbodhi* or *Khamāj*). Any time, love.

S G M P D n S̄ S̄ n D P M G R S

Jhinjhoṭī. Khamāj group. (*Cheñchuruṭṭi*). Night, love.

S R G M P D N S̄ S̄ n D P M G R S

Tilaṅga. Khamāj group. Night, quiet.

S G M P N S̄ S̄ n P M G S

IV. *Bhairava.* (*Māyāmālavagauḷa*). Dawn, reverence.

S r G M P d N S̄

Jogiyā. Bhairava group. (*Sāverī*). Dawn, adoration.

S r̄ M P D̄ S̄ S̄ N D̄ P M G r S

Lalitā. Bhairava group. (*Sūryakāntā*). Night, tenderness.

S r G M m d N Ṡ

V. *Pūrvī*. (*Kāmavardhanī*). Evening, mystery.

S r G M m P d N Ṡ

In the United Provinces both varieties of Dha are used. M is only a passing note.

Śrīrāga. Pūrvī group. Sunset, mystery and contemplation.

S r m P d N Ṡ Ṡ N d P m G r S

Gaurī. Pūrvī group. Afternoon, laughter.

S r m P N Ṡ Ṡ N d P m G r S

VI. *Mārvā*. (*Gamanapriyā*.) Afternoon, love and passion.

S r G m D N Ṡ

G is occasionally the aṁśa of this *rāga*.

Hindol. Mārvā group. Evening, calm and joy.

S G m D N Ṡ

Some say that the aṁśa note is Dha. There are many varieties of Hindol in use.

VII. *Kāphī.* (*Kharaharapriyā*). Morning, passion.

S R g M P D n Ṡ

Dhanāśrī. Kāphī group. Afternoon, calm.

S g M P n Ṡ Ṡ n D P M g R S

This variety is very common in western India.

Bhīmpalāsī. Kāphī group. Afternoon, quiet.

S g M P n Ṡ Ṡ n D P M g R S

Sāraṅga. Kāphī group. (*Madhyamāvatī*). Noon, contemplation and illusion.

S R M P D n N Ṡ

VIII. *Āsāvarī.* (*Naṭabhairavī*). Evening, tenderness.

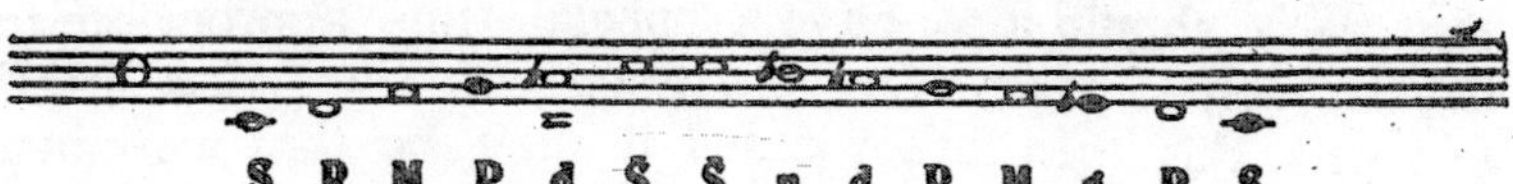

S R M P d Ṡ Ṡ n d P M g R S

Gāndhārī. Āsāvarī group. (*Gandhārava*). Evening.

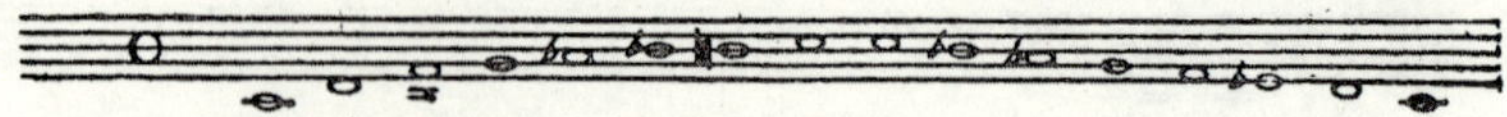

S R M P d n N Ṡ Ṡ n d P M g R S

IX. *Bhairavī*. (*Hanumatoḍī*). Morning, sad.

S r g M P d n Ṡ

The Aṁśa varies between M and d.

Mālkos. Bhairavī group. (*Also called Mālakauṅśa*). Night, laughter.

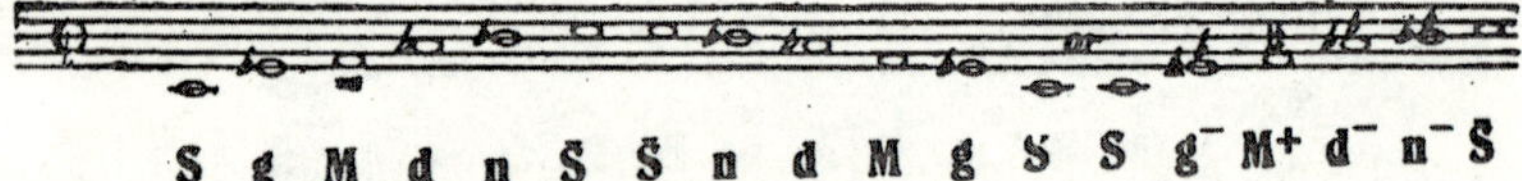

S g M d n Ṡ Ṡ n d M g S S g^{-} M^{+} d^{-} n^{-} S

This is one of the popular northern rāgas

X. *Toḍī*. (*Śubhapantuvarāḷī*). Morning, adoration.

S r g m P d N Ṡ S r^{-} g^{-} m^{+} P d^{-} N^{+} S

Multānī. Toḍī group. Evening, calm.

S G m P N Ṡ Ṡ N d P m g r S g^{-} m^{+} r d^{-}

Another important matter is the time of day at which different *rāgas* should be sung. Each *rāga* is connected with a special mood or passion, and it is therefore fitting that each should also have a special time appropriate to it. In some cases the character of the *rāga* itself explains this. In other cases it may be that we must seek the explanation in historical facts connected with each *rāga*, or in the division of the day into auspicious and inauspicious periods, which still determines so greatly the life of the Hindu household.

The musical character of the different *rāgas* also suggests certain explanations, which have been very carefully worked out by Mr. Bhatkhande for Hindusthani *rāgas*. The four determinant musical factors for the time theory according to him are the following: the position of the *aṁśa*, the presence or absence of *Tīvra Ma*, of *Komal* and *Tīvra śrutis*, and the omission of certain *svaras*.

The day is divided into the following periods:—

1. *Sandhiprakāś*, both morning and evening, the conjunction of dark and light, i.e. sunrise and sunset, between 4–7, both a.m. and p.m.

2. Before and after *Sandhiprakāś*, from 10–4 and 7–10, both a.m. and p.m.

This gives altogether six periods in the twenty-four hours. He works out the following principles:—

1. *Rāgas* having *Ri Komal* and *Ga Tīvra* are *Sandhiprakāś rāgas*, i.e. the *Bhairava*, *Pūrvī* and *Mārvā* groups.

2. *Rāgas* having *Ri Suddha*, *Dha Śuddha*, and *Ga Śuddha* come after the *Sandhiprakāś*, i.e. the *Bilāval*, *Kalyāṇī* and *Khamāj* groups.

3. *Rāgas* having *Ga Komal* and *Ni Komal* come before *Sandhiprakāś*, i.e. the *Kāphī*, *Bhairavī* and *Āsāvarī* groups.

The question as to whether the *rāga* should come in the first or the second half of the day is decided by two factors, the position of the *aṁśa*, and the use of *Tīvra Ma*.

4. *Rāgas* having their *aṁśa* in the first tetrachord (*Pūrvāṅga*) come between noon and midnight. They are called *Pūrva rāgas*.

5. *Rāgas* having their *aṁśa* in the second tetrachord (*Uttarāṅga*) come between midnight and noon. They are called *Uttara rāgas*.

Ma and *Pa* are not counted as in either tetrachord.

6. *Ma Tīvra* also gives an indication of the time of the *rāga*. For this reason it is called *Adhvadarśak*, or

'showing the way.' It comes in the evening *Sandhi* group and continues into the next group. It does not, however, occur in the morning groups, unless attended by a dominant *Komal Ma* in a few of the early morning *rāgas*, e.g. *Hindol*. The only *rāgas* sung during the day and taking *Ma Tīvra* are *Toḍī*, *Gaur-sāraṅga*, *Multānī*; and there is some doubt about these. Skilful musicians sometimes introduce *Ma Tīvra* as a passing note into other night *rāgas*, without in any way offending musical susceptibilities.

7. An additional indication of time is found in the transilient *rāgas*. Evening *rāgas* do not as a rule omit *Ga* and *Ni* altogether, and morning *rāgas* do not omit *Ri* and *Dha*.

In the south, the time theory is largely a matter of tradition, and while many of these principles apply, the subject has not been carefully worked out.

Many interesting anecdotes are related which bear on this time theory. It is said that once the celebrated Tān Sen was ordered by the Emperor to sing a night *rāga* at noon. As he sang, darkness came down on the place where he stood, and spread around as far as the sound reached.

There are other fanciful aspects of the *rāga* system which have to be taken into account. It must always be remembered that in Indian melodies the mood or flavour is of primal importance; and so many things, which appear to the West to be merely fanciful, are important factors for the music of the East.

The root meaning of *rāga* is 'passion', and from very ancient times each *rāga* has been associated with particular passions and emotions. Rājah Sir S. M. Tagore thus describes the passions to be associated with the six principal *rāgas* he enumerates:—

1. *Śrīrāga* is to be sung in the dewy season, and represents love. 2. *Vasanta* is the *rāga* of the spring, and is allied with the emotion of joy. 3. *Bhairava* is the *rāga* of asceticism and reverence. 4. *Pañchamā* is the *rāga* of the calm night. 5. *Megh* is the *rāga* of the rainy season and is allied with the emotion of exuberant joy, such as the

coming of the rainy season means to so many in India. 6. *Naṭṭanārāyaṇa* is the *rāga* of battle and fierce courage.

Here is another interesting description, from the pen of an accomplished southern musician, of the emotions associated with the different *rāgas*. 'All the permutations and combinations are performed on the basis of the notes of which the *rāga* is primarily composed and any deviations are looked upon as discordant and are scrupulously guarded against. *Toḍī* and *Bhairavī* represent majesty and impress one like the march of a stately king, decked in all his regal glory and spreading the pomp and circumstance of his lofty position, a grand and sublime spectacle. *Āsāvarī* and *Punnāgavarāḷī* are wrapped in melancholy, like one pleading the cause of a sovereign unjustly deposed from his throne and power. *Gīrvāṇī* and *Vasanta* come serene and subdued, like a sage sitting in a lonely forest or on a mountain, calmly contemplating the beauty of the universe. *Mōhana* and *Pūrvakalyāṇī* appear like a coy maiden hiding her love, as a rose does its blooming petals beneath its bower of green, but withal conscious of its beauty and attractiveness. *Husenī* seems fascinating in its sadness, like a maiden estranged from her lover or spurned by him, cursing the woeful hour which parted her from his company, or eloquently pleading the justice of her cause. *Bihāgaḍā* comes arguing and resentful and remonstrating. *Nādanāmakriyā*, calm and thoughtful, appears like Socrates or Plato preaching the sublime truths of philosophy to his disciples. *Nīlāmbari* and *Yadukulakāmbodhi* come submissive and imploring, melting the soul into streams of tender devotion, like a true *bhakta* full of prayers and tears in the presence of God. Thus each *rāga* comes and goes with its store of smiles or tears, of passion or pathos, its noble and lofty impulses, and leaves its mark on the mind of the hearer.' [1]

It is noted that the sadder *rāgas* have an average of three flats as against an average of two flats for those which picture the more joyous emotions.

[1] Lakshmana Pillay, I.M.J., pp. 71, 72.

5

Indian *rāgas* are also supposed to be able to reproduce the conditions and emotions associated with them. The *Dīpak rāga* is supposed to produce flames in actuality ; and a story is told of a famous musician named Naik Gopāl who, when ordered to sing this by the Emperor Akbar, went and stood in the Jumna up to his neck and then started the song. The water became gradually hotter until it was boiling, and he went on singing until flames burst out of his body and he was consumed to ashes. The *Megh mallār rāga* is supposed to be able to produce rain. It is said that a dancing girl in Bengal, in a time of drought, once drew from the clouds with this *rāga* a timely refreshing shower which saved the rice crop. Sir W. Ousley, who relates many of these anecdotes, says that he was told by Bengal people that this power of reproducing the actual conditions of the *rāga* is now only possessed by some musicians in western India, and by people in western India that such musicians can only be found in Bengal.

There are many interesting anecdotes told with reference to *rāgas*. One of these relates a story of a southern musician named Toḍī Sītārāmāyya,—so-called on account of his fondness for the *rāga Toḍī*,—who was a musician at the court of the Mahārāja Sarabhoji of Tanjore in the last century. The musician got into serious money difficulties, and was forced by the money lender to whom he went to mortgage his favourite *rāga Toḍī* for the loan he obtained, under the condition that until the money was repaid he should not sing it before any one. It was not long before Sarabhoji missed his favourite *rāga* and asked his musician to sing it. He explained why he could not do so ; and then the Mahārāja laughed heartily at the cuteness of the moneylender and paid up the loan, besides rewarding the moneylender for his keen appreciation of the value of music. Another story is told of a prince, who was not possessed of sufficient musical knowledge to recognize the different *rāgas* when they were played or sung, and so arranged with a princess, who was well versed in music, to help him by means of a special prompting apparatus. This consisted of a set of strings, hardly visible at a distance, suspended from above, directly opposite the principal organs of the prince's face. Whenever a *rāga* was sung before him, the princess, who was sitting in an upper chamber where she could manipulate the strings, would pull the appropriate string opposite the organ representing the *rāga* sung. Thus for *Kāmbodhi* the ear (*kādu*) string was pulled, for *Mukhārī* the nose (*mūkku*) string, for *Kānaḍā* the eye (*kaṇṇu*) string and so on. So the prince was able to show off his skill in naming the particular *rāgas*. One day, however, the princess in her excitement pulled the springs so hastily, that the whole apparatus fell down, and the prince, who could no longer name the *rāgas*, had to retire ashamed from the Durbar.

In connection with the science of *rāga*, Indian music has developed the art of *rāga* pictures. Principal Percy Brown of the School of Art, Calcutta, defines a *rāga* as 'a work of art in which the tune, the song, the picture, the colours, the season, the hour and the virtues are so blended together as to produce a composite production to which the west can furnish no parallel.' It may be described as a musical movement, which is not only represented by sound, but also by a picture. Rajah S. M. Tagore thus describes the pictorial representations of his six principal *rāgas*. *Śrīrāga* is represented as a divine being wandering through a beautiful grove with his love, gathering fragrant flowers as they pass along. Near by, doves sport on the grassy sward. *Vasanta rāga*, or the *rāga* of spring, is represented as a young man of golden hue, standing in a mango grove, dressed in yellow garments, and having his ears ornamented with mango blossoms, some of which he also holds in his hands. 'His lotus-like eyes are rolling round and are of the colour of the rising sun. He is loved by the females.' *Bhairava* is shown as the great Mahādeva (Śiva) seated as a sage on a mountain top. Gaṅgā falls upon his matted locks. His head is adorned with the crescent moon. In the centre of his forehead is the third eye from which issued the flames which reduced Kāma, the Indian Cupid, to ashes. Serpents twine round his body which gleams with sacred ashes smeared all over it. He holds a trident in one hand and a skull in the other. Before him stands the sacred bull. *Pañchamā rāga* is pictured as a very young couple, fondling one another on a grassy sward in the midst of a forest. The *rāga* itself is represented by a young man who has large red eyes and wears red clothes. *Megh* is the *rāga* of the clouds and the rainy season. Clouds stretch across the sky, and lightning flashes pierce them. Seated upon a royal elephant, with his bride at his side, is the splendid young king who represents this *rāga.* He is dressed in blue garments, or is shown as blue in colour, like the mighty Indra. 'He has a grave voice and violet eyes.' *Naṭṭanārāyaṇa* is the *rāga* of battle. A warrior king rides on a galloping steed over the field of battle, with lance and bow and shield. Dead bodies of the slain lie round about. Blood streams from his body.

Some time ago Principal Percy Brown read a paper on this subject which he called 'Visualized Music'. He described it as a combination of the two arts, music and painting. He mentioned a miniature painting which was called 'the fifth delineation of the melody *Megh Mallār Sāraṅga*, played in four-time at the time of the spring rains.' There are a large number of such paintings, all having some reference to a prescribed tune, performed under conditions defined by some specified season. Many of these may be seen in the Art Gallery of the Indian Museum, Calcutta ; and the India Office, London, has a fine collection. The art seems to have come originally from north-west India. It is not known, however, how it originated ; or whether it belongs to India or came from Persia. The Indian tendency is to visualize abstract things, and so it is quite possible that it was Indian in origin. Principal Brown mentions that experiments have been made at Manchester University by Professor Dalbe as to the connection between music and colour. There is a school in London where music is taught in association with colour, each scale having its own peculiar colour scheme. It is evident therefore that this connection is not merely sentimental. Principal Percy Brown in the lecture referred to gives the following description of some of these *rāga* pictures. '*Toḍī rāgiṇī* is one of the brides of *Vasanta rāga*. The melody of this *rāga* is so fascinating that

Picture of Kedāra rāga

From Johnson Collection, India Office, London

every living creature within hearing is attracted by it. As the *rāga* has to be performed at midday, the picture shows a nymph standing in an open landscape in the brilliant noonday sun, clothed in a snow-white *sāri* and perfumed with the camphor of Kashmīr. In her hands she holds the *vīṇā*, and all the deer in the neighbouring pastures stand entranced as she plays. The musician, as he plays, is supposed to conjure up before his audience the scene of the picture, the charm of the nymph, the beauty of her costume, the langurous scent of the blossoms, mingled with the faint odour of camphor, and the rustling sound of the animals as they advance enthralled. One is reminded of the stories of Chopin playing before the boys in such a way, that they saw all the scenes which were in his mind as he played. The *Sāraṅga* melody pictures the glare of the desert, and the heat-waves rising and falling with the mirage of the cool refreshing stream in the distance, and the thirsty black buck galloping towards the oasis, or sobbing out its wrath on the burning sand as it realizes the hopelessness of the search. *Pañchamā* is shown by a picture of a shower in the hot weather and a band of musicians who express their appreciation of the rain. The thunder-clouds hover overhead and the lightning strikes through the sky. Peacocks spread out their tails and call in joy, and frogs sit around and croak. The god Kṛishṇa of dark blue colour stalks around. The leaf buds of the trees show new red shoots ; the cattle hold up their heads refreshed, the herdsman standing by. Waterfowl gather round the parched pool, and overhead a horde of white herons fly across.' This subject of 'Visualized Music' is quite an untrodden path, and it is hoped that others will follow where Professor Brown points. A collection of all the *rāga* pictures in existence would be a very good beginning. Mr. Fox Strangways notes that the Chippewa Indians of North America also draw pictures of their tunes, by the help of which they may be sung.

Kedāra rāga, the picture of which faces this page, is represented as a group of musicians playing and singing in the moonlight. The lotus buds are all closed. There is gaiety and sadness combined in the picture. It is the dewy season, and it is believed that while the *rāga* means gaiety to-day, it means also sadness in the future. The ascetic in the group typifies the illusoriness of the present.

Megh rāga, in the frontispiece, is represented by a group of musicians playing outside a fine house in the daytime during the rainy season. It is a *rāga* of hope and new life. The clouds hang overhead, and already some drops of rain have fallen. The animals in the fields rejoice. The background of the picture is deep blue, with a rich band of brown. This *rāga* is said to be helpful for patients suffering from tuberculosis.

CHAPTER V

TĀLA OR TIME MEASURES

MUSICAL time in India, more obviously than elsewhere, is a development from the prosody and metres of poetry. The insistent demands of language and the idiosyncrasies of highly characteristic verse haunt the music, like a 'presence which is not to be put by.' 'The time-relations of music are affected both by the structure of the language and by the method of versification which ultimately derives from it,' says one student of Indian music from the west. Until the nineteenth century, there was practically no prose in India and everything was learnt through the medium of verse chanted to regular rules. Both in Sanskrit and in the vernaculars all syllables are classified according to their time-lengths, the unit of time being a *mātra*. Very short syllables of less than a *mātra* also occur.

Great stress has always been laid by Indian grammarians upon giving the 'exact value' to syllables in verse; and as there is no accent at all in Indian verse, the time-length is all important. This may account for the great development of time-measures in Indian music. The different time-measures for verse are most carefully laid down and have to be strictly adhered to. When grammar, philosophy, history and geography are learnt in verse, one gets the sense of duration and rhythm highly developed, and it is this sense of duration that is the central thing in Indian time. Any one who studies Indian prosody can easily see the great difficulty, to say the least, of obtaining a pleasurable result by combining Indian verse with western tunes. One of the most difficult things for the foreigner to get away from in an Indian vernacular is the stressing of syllables. The division into words is not at all important in Indian verse, and so music does not take particular note of this. In India words are more often set to music, rather than music to words. It is easy to see then the importance of time-measure in Indian music. The westerner often finds these time-measures far more difficult to master than the melodies, strange though those often are. The varieties of time-measure may be somewhat imperfectly realized by listening to the rythmical beats of the drum in some distant village on a quiet moonlight night, when all other sounds are stilled and one can get the full benefit of this one sound. Sometimes one hears beats arranged in bars like this :

| 2. 1. 1. | 2. 1. 1. | 2. 1. 1. | 2. 1. 1. |

or again,

| 1. 2. | 1. 2. | 1. 2. | 1. 2. | 1. 2. |

or again,

| 2. 3. | 2. 3. | 2. 3. | 2. 3. | 2. 3. |

or again,

| 7. 1. 2. | 7. 1. 2. | 7. 1. 2. | 7. 1. 2. |

Such an exercise will not only help one to appreciate the rhythmic soul of India and the intricacy of Indian time, but will also help to pass the hours when one is forced to lie awake.

Though the nomenclature varies, as might be expected, the theory of *tāla* (as time-measure is called) in the north and south is more uniform than that of *rāga*. As usual, a fanciful origin must be found for *tāla*. It is said that Bharata discovered the thirty-two kinds of *tāla* in the song of the lark. Raja S. M. Tagore says that the word *tāla* refers to the beating of time by the clapping of hands. Sometimes it is also done by means of small hand-cymbals, which are called *tāla* or *kaitāla* or *kartāl* (hand-cymbals). It may be that, as has been suggested, the main difficulty for westerners in realizing and enjoying the nice distinctions of Indian rhythm is that they have not acquired the habit of resolving mentally every unit into its consutuent elements, so that they could sing them at a moment's notice.

Mr. Fox Strangways, elaborating the difference between Indian and European time-measures, says:

'Indian rhythm moves in āvartas (bars) broken up into vibhāgas (beats), each of which contains one or more *tālas*. We can equally say of ours that it moves in sections broken up into bars, each of which contains one or more beats. In what does the difference between the two systems consist? It may be answered that theirs is derived from song, ours from the dance or the march: that both are based on the numbers two and three, but that they add and we multiply in order to form combinations of these. But the answer which goes deepest is that their music is in modes of time (as we saw that it was in modes of tune), and that ours changes that mode at will, principally by means of harmony. In order that rhythm, an articulation of the infinite variety of sounds, may be upon some regular plan, the plan must have some recognizable unit of measurement. India takes the short note and gives it, for a particular rhythm, a certain value as opposed to the long; Europe takes the stressed note and gives it in a particular rhythm a certain frequency, as against the unstressed, and graduates its force. We find the unity of the rhythm in the recurrent bar (which is always in double or triple time, just as our two melodic modes are either major or minor), and have to look elsewhere for the variety; they find variety in the vibhāga, whose constitution is extremely various, and must look elsewhere for the large spaces of time; they find unity in the āvarta, and we find variety in the sections.' 'Indian rhythms have their raison d'être in the contrast of long and short duration, and to identify these with much or little stress is to vulgarize the rhythms. Stress pulses and demands regularity; duration is complementary and revels in irregularity. In order to get the true sense of duration we have to get rid of stress.'[1]

The value which Indian music attaches to time may be judged from a description of a certain musician as 'an excellent timist,' and from the name of sextuple Govinda Nair given to a musician of Travancore, on account of his great skill in singing in sextuple accelerated time. One can hardly imagine such terms being used in the west.

Musical time is based upon the *akshara* or syllable. Five main note lengths are recognized, made up of a different number of *aksharas*. They are.

Anudruta	... 1 Akshara	... $\frac{1}{4}$ Mātra
Druta	... 2 ,,	... $\frac{1}{2}$,,
Laghu	... 4 ,,	... 1 ,,
Guru	... 8 ,,	... 2 ,,
Pluta	...12 ,,	... 3 ,,
Kākapāda	...16 ,,	... 4 ,,

[1] *Music of Hindusthan*, pp. 217, 218.

One āvarta or section contains from 2 to 4 bars or vibhāgas, each of which is constituted by a number of angas (members), consisting of one or more of these time units. The virāma or rest is used for lengthening the druta and laghu by any fraction.

Each āvarta must begin the time-measure correctly, and all the various time elaborations must be worked out in the āvarta.

The *Saṅgīta-Ratnākara* gives 120 examples of different time-measures, formed by the combination of these time-units, the bar varying in length from one to nineteen notes. Most of these are very unlike any of the *tāla* employed to-day, and so there is nothing gained by discussing them. We shall therefore take up the time system as it is to-day in both northern and southern music. Here again there is a good deal of difference between the north and the south. Many of the times are the same, but the names and the method of classification are different. As with *rāga*, so here also, the south has a very much more systematic classification than the north. According to Carnatic music, there are seven *tālas*, each of which has five jātis or classes. The five jātis are classified according to the number of *aksharas* in the principal aṅga. These are said to correspond to the five castes, and their origin is traced to the five faces of Īśvara. Naṭarāja (Śiva) is supposed to have worked these out in his wonderful dance, while Brahma played the hand-cymbals and Vishṇu the *mṛidaṅga*. This would certainly have been a band worth going far to see and hear. The five jātis are named after the number of *aksharas* in the principal beat, viz. *trisra* for three, *chatusra* for four, *khaṇḍa* for five, *miśra* for seven and *saṅkīrṇa* for nine. It is interesting to see that, with the exception of the second, all the other numbers are odd, the times being mostly combinations of two and an odd number. The same thing is found in Hindusthani *tāla*. The other aṅgas of the āvarta have either one or two *aksharas*. The following is a table of the *tālas* as they are arranged in the Carnatic system. It will be noticed that they are not arranged in the order of the number in the principal beat, but in the usual Indian method of arranging them, and the reason given is that columns 1 and 2, when added up make column 3, and 1 and 4 make column 5. There is probably a further reason in the fact that the four *akshara* time is the more common.

NAME	1 Cha-tusra	2 Trisra	3 Miśra	4 Khaṇḍa	5 Saṅkīr-na
1. Eka tāla ...	4	3	7	5	9
2, Rūpaka tāla ...	2.4	2.3	2.7	2.5	2.9
3. Jhampa tāla ...	4.1.2	3.1.2.	7.1.2.	5.1.2.	9.1.2
4. Tripuṭa tāla ...	4.2.2	3.2.2.	7.2.2.	5.2.2.	9.2.2.
5. Mathya tāla ...	4.2.4	3.2.3.	7.2.7.	5.2.5.	9.2.9
6. Dhruva tāla ...	4.2.4.4	3.2.3.3.	7.2.7.7.	5.2.5.5.	9.2.9.9.
7. Aṭa tāla ...	4.4.2.2.	3.3.2.2.	7.7.2.2.	5.5.2.2.	9.9.2.2.

The table shows that in *eka tāla* there is only one aṅga in each vibhāga, in *rūpaka* there are two, in *jhampa, tripuṭa* and *maṭhya* there are three, and in the last two four. The name *eka tāla* by itself is usually given to the *chatusra jāti*, and the name *rūpaka tāla* without prefix also refers to the *chatusra jāti*. In *jhampa tāla* the *miśra jāti* has the simple name, and in *tripuṭa tāla* the *trisra jāti*. In *maṭhya* and *dhruva tāla* it is the *chatusra jāti* which takes the simple name, but in *aṭa tāla* the *khaṇḍa jāti* has it. These are all underlined in the table, so that they may be clearly seen. The name *ādi tāla* is usually given to the *chatusra jāti* of *tripuṭa tāla*, as this is one of the commonest *tālas* of southern music.

The *āvarta*, as we have seen, is made up of a number of *vibhāgas*. One of these takes the principal beat and one of them has no beat at all. The former is called the *sam* in the north and *mirtāy* in the south. The beat before the *sam* is called the *khāli*, because it is the custom to show it by an empty wave of the hand. These beats are very important and the musicians have to keep them in mind, otherwise the time will go astray.

In Hindusthani music the time-measures are arranged somewhat differently. We have first *eka tāla* of the *chatusra* variety, and none of the other *jātis* are used. In *rūpaka tāla*, only the *chatusra* (2. 4) and *trisra* (2. 3) *jātis* are found. There is also another kind of *rūpaka tāla* which has three angas, thus 3. 2. 2. *Jhampa tāla* in the north runs 2. 3. 2. 3.—a kind of doubled *rūpaka*. There is also another kind of *jhampa* which goes 3. 3. 2. 2. In *tripuṭa tāla* we find the *trisra* and *chatusra jātis*. The former goes 3. 2. 2 and is called *tevrā*. The latter is called *tītāla*, *tīntāl*, or *trītāla*—three-beat—and also *kavālī* in Bengal. There is also another kind of *tītāla* which goes 4. 4. 4. 4 with the *sam* on the third beat. *Maṭhya tāla* is represented by its *chatusra jāti*, which is called *sūlaphākatā tāla* or *surphākatā*, meaning 'zigzag'. Sometimes it runs 2. 4. 4 instead of 4. 2. 4. *Dhruva tāla* is represented by its *chatusra jāti* which is called *aṭa-chautāla* and has two forms: 4. 2. 4. 4 and 2. 4. 4. 4, the *sam* being on the first *mātra*. The word *aṭa-chautāla* means 'crooked four-beat time.' This time is used a great deal in dhrupads. *Aṭa tāla* has three *jātis* in the north, viz. *chautāla* 4. 4. 2. 2., *jhampa tāla* 3. 3. 2. 2., *dhamār tāla* 5. 5. 4.

There are also a number of times which correspond to none of the regular southern times. These include the following :—

Farodast. 2. 2. 4. 4 or 2. 2. 2. 3. 4.

Dhīma tāla, also called in the north *ādi tāla*, 4. 4. 4. 4, with the *sam* on the first beat.

Dādrā, also called *pashto*—a syncopated *tāla* especially used with the *dādrā* class of song. It runs 3. 3 with the *sam* on the first note.

Jhumrā. 3. 4. 3. 4. It has the *sam* on the first beat. This is a very popular time-measure.

Most of these irregular times were introduced by the Muhammadans.

There is also an irregular southern time called *chāpu tāla.* It has two varieties, either trisra or miśra, viz. 1. 2. or 1. 2. 2. 2. *Chāpu tāla* is used a great deal in folk songs. It is, as may easily be seen, a syncopated time.

South Indian time experts reckon that there are altogether 108 different varieties of tāla possible by means of various ingenious combinations. Most of them, it need hardly be said, are not in use, though occasionally some expert technician accomplishes a *tour de force* away from the beaten track of time-measures; as when Subramanāyyar sang a piece in the *Simhanandana tāla,* which is one of the most complicated. The bar signature of this tāla runs as follows: 8. 8. 4. 8. 4. 8. 2. 2. 8. 8. 4. 8. 4. 8. 8. 4. 4 or 100 *aksharas.* This musician it may be surmised was a prodigy in South Indian time experts.

As in western music, so in India, it is possible to include in the *akshara* two, three, or even more shorter notes. These are called *kalai.* Their inclusion does not alter the time, but renders the singing or playing of the piece more difficult. It means that the longer notes may be broken up into shorter ones, and so on, till the ability of the performer is exhausted. A singer of Travancore was known as Shaṭkāla Govinda Mārar, because he could sing anything in sextuple time. In all this manipulation of time-measure, the main elements of the time must be retained throughout and the *rāga* must be adhered to.

The clapping of the hands is much used in India to indicate time. There are different signs used for the different beats, so as to make quite clear what kind of time is used. The first note of a beat is indicated by a clap. This may be followed either by the counting of the other *aksharas* with the fingers or by a wave. If the beat is a laghu, that is one of more than two *aksharas,* then the other units are shown by counting with the separate fingers on the palm of the other hand. If the beat is a druta of two *aksharas* only, then the extra unit is shown by a wave of the hand. For example,

Ādi tāla runs

× ' ' ' × ᔕ × ᔕ
1 2 3 4 / 5 6 / 7 8

Rūpaka tāla

× ᔕ × ' ' '
1 2 / 3 4 5 6

× means a clap, ' counting with fingers, and ᔕ a wave.

This is one of the easiest ways to learn Indian time, and one can soon get into the way of singing to it.

There are three different speeds in Indian time. They are slow-*vilamba kāla*, medium-*madhya kāla*, quick-*druta kāla*. These will correspond roughly to Adagio, Moderato, and Allegro. The names used in the north for these are *bilampet*, *joru*, and *durt*. *Dūṇ* is used for very quick time.

Drumming

As we have seen in the sketch of the History of Indian music, the drum is one of the most important of Indian musical instruments, and so it demands special treatment in accordance with ancient practice. The ordinary Indian drummer earns far more than the school teacher with twice his education. He also spends it more quickly. The following quotation from an English author will help to make clear the place of drumming in Indian music.

'The drum is used not, as with us, to assert the accent at special moments, or to reinforce a crisis, but to articulate the metre of the singer's melody, or to add variety to it by means of a cross metre. There are four main elements in drumming; the quality, the intensity, the pitch of the sounds, and the time intervals between them. We do not, on the whole, use percussion much. When we do, we value it, perhaps, chiefly for the graduated intensity with which it points the rhythm. We look a little askance at varieties of quality; we recognize the drums, the cymbals, and the triangle; but we are not quite sure how far the tambourine, castanets, and Berlioz's flannel-headed drumsticks are legitimate music. Of the pitch we only demand that it should not clash with other sounds. It is in no way a vital constituent of the harmony, which is almost invariably complete without it. The time intervals of the drum notes reinforce as a whole those of the other instruments; they seldom cross them, and only produce a certain amount of confusion when they do, which however may be a useful resource upon occasion.

In Indian music the graduated intensity of the sound is very little regarded, either in singing or playing or in drumming, because their whole scheme is not accentual but quantitative. It is true that the first of the bar is often louder than the rest, but not always; but this is not in order that it may, as with us, stand out against other accents; but because two quantitative schemes are apt to coincide there, and two sounds are louder than one. The time intervals are with them all important, and show great variety; it is seldom that more than a few bars, out of hundreds, are drummed in exactly the same way. And the drumming is practically continuous; it is only occasionally silenced for special contrast. The pitch again is all important, for it is invariably the keynote, and frequently the drum is the singer's only accompaniment. Lastly, a maximum of variety is got into the quality; and this not mainly by the variety of the instruments. For though there are scores of shapes for drums, tambourines, cymbals, triangles and so forth, they are not usually assembled together, because concerted music is the exception, not the rule. The variety is got out of the drum, or the pair of drums themselves. They are played with the full hand and the fingers, rarely with sticks; there are half a dozen strokes for the right hand and three or four for the left. Of these Lady Wilson's drummer said, 'The beat with the left hand is like the seam of my coat, that must be there; the other notes with the right hand are like the embroidery I may put according to my own fancy over the seam.' These 'notes' are differentiated not by pitch, but by quality. They are also articulated by great intricacy of time-interval. For neither of these two things has our music any real analogues; and the Bengālis do not overstate the case in their saying, 'Yantrapatir Mṛidaṅga,' 'the drum is the lord of instruments.'[1]

The various kinds of drum are described in chapter vii; so here we shall only take up the discussion of the practice of drumming on the mṛidaṅga or the tablā. These two are the same in principle and are the drums used throughout India for the accompaniment of vocal music.

The mridaṅga and tablā are both played in the same way, the only difference being that, in the case of the tablā, the two heads are on two small drums and not on the same drum. The right hand note of the drum is the keynote—the *Shaḍja*—and the left hand note a lower *Pa.* Exact tuning is very important, as the slightest difference will be evident and will spoil the melody, the drum being the principal accompaniment for the singer.

[1] *Music of Hindusthan*, pp. 225, 226.

The right hand plays the first beat of each vibhāga with the ball of the finger tips. The base of the hand is pressed on the drumhead, and the rest of the hand is curved so that the finger tips strike easily. The left hand shows the end of the bar and strikes, sometimes with the whole palm, and sometimes with the lower palm and fingers. Sometimes it moves across the parchment, giving a strange sound 'like a galosh leaving the mud,' curious but by no means unattractive. The drummer constantly varies the method of beating the *aksharas* in the bar. The total number must be constant and the left-hand strike must always come in at the exact moment; but outside these the drummer has the possibility of infinite variety, and expert drummers use it to the utmost. The singer depends upon the drummer to keep him to the time. He may go off into all kinds of extempore pieces and flourishes, leaving, as it seems, for the moment all semblance of time, but the thought is always there and again he will come back to it. Mrs. Mann says,

> 'The Indian drummer is a great artist. He will play a rhythm concerto all alone and play us into an ecstacy with it.'
>
> The drummer will play it in bars of 10, 13, 16, or 20 beats, with divisions within each bar flung out with a marvellous hypnotizing swing. Suggestions of such rhythm beaten out by a ragged urchin on the end of an empty kerosene oil-can first aroused me to the beauty and power of Indian music.'

The Indian drummer can obtain the most fascinating rhythm from a mud pot, and some of them are great experts at this pot-drumming.

The drummer is most particular about the ending of the drumming. This must always be on the Sam. The singer also ends here, and after going off into a kind of recitative, he will watch for the drummer and come back so as to end on the Sam. In the south, the treatment is somewhat different, and the Mirtāy is often on the second beat. The principal notes of the *rāga*, that is the Vādī and Saṁvādī notes, are usually placed on the Sam beat. This also indicates to the audience where they should applaud. The Khāli is the wave-of-the-hand-beat and helps the singer to determine the Sam. It shows him when the Sam is coming, as the drummer is silent on this beat. The

Khāli always comes just before the Sam, so that, however lost the singer may be in his improvisation, the Khāli shows him the way back to the Sam.

Drummers have a curious system of mnemonics, which tell them how the drum accompaniment should be beaten out. These are composed of syllables, each of which indicates one particular kind of beat and also the nature of the *tāla* as a whole. The actual syllables used vary in different parts of India but the following are some of them :—

NORTHERN

Tritāla 4.4.4.4.

1	2	+	3
Tā Dhīn Dhīn tā	Tā Dhīn Dhīn tā	Tā Tīn Tīn tā	Tā Dhīn Dhīn tā

Rūpaka 3.2.2.

+	2	3
Dhīn Dhā Trik	Dhīn Dhīn	Dhā Trik

Jhampa 2.3.2.3.

+	2	0	3
Dhīn na	Dhīn Dhīn na	Tīn na	Dhīn dhīn na

Chautāla 4.4.2.2.

+	0	2	0	3	
Ḍhā dhā	Dhīn ta	Kit Dha	Dhīn ta	Kit tak	gadigina

+ indicates the *sam* and 0 the *khāli* beat.

In these mnemonics, or bōls, as they are called, the following are to be played by the right hand: Dhīn, Nā, Tā, Trik, Tīn, it, ki. The following by the left hand: Dha, Ta. The following are played by both hands together: Dhā, Dhīn.

6

The southern arrangement is somewhat different and runs thus:

Āditāla 4.2.2.

	1	0	2	3
(1)	Tā	ti	Nām	Tōm

Tā—by the left hand with four fingers.
ti—by the right hand with four fingers on the middle of drum.
Nām—by the left with all fingers.
Tom—by both hands with all fingers at once.

	+	0	2	
(2)	Tadimi	Takitta	Tām	i.e. 2.2.4

Ta—by right hand first finger on the border of drum.
di—by the left middle finger.
mi—by the right middle finger on the middle of drum.
ki—as mi.
tta—as ta.
Tām—by both hands simultaneously.

	+	0	2	3
(3)	Takitta	tikitta	Tōnkitta	Nāmkitta

Ta—by the left with all fingers and right with forefinger on the border.
ki—by right with middle finger.
tta—by right with forefinger on border.
ti—by left with four fingers.
Ton—by both hands with all fingers.
Nām—as Ton.

Rūpaka 2.4.2.4.

0	1	0	~
Talangu	Tōm	Talangu	Tāy

Ta—by left hand.
lan—by right with second finger on border.
gu—by middle finger.
Tom—by both hands with all fingers.
Tāy—as Tom.

Quite a number of these curious and interesting mnemonics will be found in Mr. Fox Strangways' book, *The Music of Hindosthan*, pp. 228, 245.

CHAPTER VI

MUSICAL COMPOSITIONS

WE have been discussing the principles of Indian music and the elements which go to make up musical compositions. We have now to see how these elements are combined into melodies. We have already seen, in the chapters on *Rāga* and *Tāla*, some of the things which give these melodies a distinctive character, and now we have to go into this more carefully. We shall notice that in regard to this matter also there is a very considerable difference between the north and the south. The general principles are the same, but all the forms and the names vary.

In the first place, we note that in Indian music generally,

> the primal unity of the Indian system is, as in the western system, in the tonic note or drone; and the sense of contrast is supplied primarily by the *aṁśa*, and the notes which are related to this as *saṁvādī*, *vivādī*, and *anuvādī*. This very contrast of the *aṁśa* and the tonic, giving as it does the peculiar character to that *rāga*, imparts unity to the melody, which thus proceeds not from necessity but from freedom.'[1]

Gamaka or Grace

This freedom is further emphasized by Grace, which in Indian music is essential, not accidental. Indian music, being without harmony, has to give a far bigger place to grace than does European music. It is the rule, rather than the exception, for the passage from one note to another to be made indirectly; and the note with its grace makes one musical utterance.

Grace in Indian music is called *gamaka*. There are said to be altogether nineteen different varieties of gamaka in existence, but some of these are hardly ever used, and the more common gamaka are about ten in number.

These strange and fascinating graces or *gamaka* have a great deal to do with the haunting beauty of Indian music.

[1] *Music of Hindosthan*, pp. 280, 281.

We hear the vīṇā or sitār player beginning with a shake, called in different parts of India, *Orikai, Varek, Mīnd*, or *Sphuritam*, and as we listen we find that it is not the ordinary shake of western music. It may begin in that way, but it becomes a wonderful shake produced by rapidly pulling the string between the frets, giving two notes whose interval may be as much as four semitones. We hear this 'deflect', as it has been called, again and again as the music proceeds, and it comes, with a sense of delightful contrast, into a melody which threatens to become monotonous. Then we hear the player trying to get the high notes and, not content with striking the note, he slides up the string to it or to the note above it, just giving us the remembrance of all the notes that lie between, so slightly as not to detract from the prominence of the note wanted, just as the breeze from some rose garden comes touched with the scent of the roses. We hear this effect frequently as the player often uses this gamaka of the *Jāru (Ghasīt, Ās, Sūkth)* as it is known. Then, as the melody begins, we shall hear the regular trill or *Kampitam*(*Kampa*), on a note here and there, and then prolonged on some important note, perhaps the aṁśa of the *rāga*. Right from the beginning we shall have found that some notes are never sounded without an *appogiatura* or leaning note, the *Humpitam*, as the Indians call it. A note that never comes in the melody itself will suddenly appear as an *appogiatura* note, or we shall hear again and again that slight sharpening and flattening of the notes which helps to fill up the blank caused by the loss of harmony. We note that the *Humpitam* is part of the music, and belongs to the note, and we learn to expect it every time that note comes. Then we hear something that is not a mere trill, nor yet a shake. Rapidly, one after the other, rising to a crescendo, we hear two notes being played, so quickly that they almost seem to mingle with one another, and yet the interval that separates them is perhaps less than a semitone or perhaps more. As it goes on, it seems almost to reach a frenzy, this *zamzamma* as it is called, and then out of it will come a beautiful phrase of the melody. As the melody develops, instead of leaping directly to a note a few semitones above, the musician will get there by a curious swing, which recurs again and again, something like **Sa Ri Sa Pa**, or two notes recurring in a swing, as **Sa Ga Sa Ga**, the third note being held just a little longer than the others. Just as the melody seems about to become monotonous by repetition, the whole thing is changed by this *Āndolitam*, as it is called. Then comes another contrast. This time the melody is struck clear by staccato notes, called fittingly *Paṭ* or *Thoṅk*. Then this also is changed, and the fingers strike flat on the sitār or vīṇā string, and give us the *Paran* notes almost like the rhythmical sound of the drum beats on the mṛidaṅga. Then, suddenly, the singer or player will go right up the scale, showing all the notes, and letting us see through what strange intervals it runs, unknown country much of it to western music. This is the *Ārohaṇa* or ascent; and the descent is called the *Avarohaṇa*, both of these being classed amongst the *gamaka*. As these are sung, we shall notice again the graced notes, these being called in the north *Mūrchhanā*, though that name is now given in the south to the *Ārohaṇa* and *Avarohaṇa* of the *rāga*. Raja S. M. Tagore says of these grace notes, 'The *Mūrchhanā* is the extending of a note to another in the ascending as well as the descending scale, without any intermediate break in the disposition of the *śrutis* in the interval', and he calls it, the essential ornament of *rāga*, without which it is as flowers without fragrance.' Again and again throughout the piece we hear these different graces, all coming just where they can produce the greatest effect, and not only depriving us of the chance of calling the music monotonous, but producing contrasting effects which add a strange beauty to it. Sometimes the slide will pass over some of the intermediate notes, and then they will tell us it is a *Līnam* and not a *Jāru*. Every grace belongs to the melody, and fits into its place without any sense of being unwanted or useless. As the melody approaches its climax, we hear the *Jhārā* and the *Boljhārā*, the melody being played slowly and clearly as a groundwork, and upon it endless arpeggio variations in accelerated time, occurring rapidly after every note, all perfectly in tune and fitting into the *rāga* framework, and bringing out the prominent notes and phrases, like an allegro variation of one of Beethoven's Sonatas, with the underlying melody making itself heard all the time. Then by *Jāru* and *Līnam*, by *Avarohaṇa* and *Ārohaṇa*, the melody comes to a close with the beat of the Sam on the drum.

Among musical compositions the simplest is the *Ālāp* or *Ālāphana*, as the northern and southern names respectively go. In this the notes of the *rāga* are sung in a loose kind of rhythm, regulated simply by convenience. It is extemporized, and is meant to notify to the audience the nature of the *rāga* which the melody will develop, and also to help the singer or player himself to get into its swing. This naturally brings out the vādī and saṁvādī notes and also the particular phrases and gamakas which belong to that *rāga*. Sometimes these *Ālāps* are called Mūrchhanā. *Ālāp* singing is one of the tests of the ability of a singer. It will often occupy about an hour, while the actual song or melody will only last for a quarter of an hour. 'Without the *Ālāp*, the listener would spend his time for some part of the song in ignorance of its tonal centres, and the melody would be for him an aimless running up and down hill; while the performer, without this little preliminary practice, would very likely play a note or two which was out of the *rāga* and so upset the unity altogether.'

In Hindusthani music the *Ālāp* is divided into three parts. There is first the *Rāg Ālāp* which shows the principal constituents of the *rāga*, that is its graha, nyāsa, vādī, saṁvādī, etc., the important notes and the notes to be lightly touched as well as the gamaka. Then, there is the *Rūpaka Ālāp* which shows the division of the piece into Astāī, Antarā, Sañchārī and Ābhog, but without words and without tāla. Then thirdly, comes the *Ākshiptikā Ālāp*, requiring both words and tāla, but still allowing a very great deal of freedom to the singer. According to the *Ratnākara*, one must begin by taking the vādī and using only three notes above that and the notes of the mandra sthāyī below. Afterwards one can go into the second tetrachord and develop that. If the vādī is in the second tetrachord, then he should begin by taking the saṁvādī or else the vādī in the mandra sthāyī. The Ālāphana is not developed in quite the same way in the south as it is in the north. It does not form such an important part of the performance, nor does it divide itself into these parts. It is simply an introduction. The different varṇa or saṅgatis take the place of this variegated Ālāp. Following the Ālāphana comes the song which may take very many forms. Then again, at the end, the music may go off into the timeless Ālāphana until it closes according to the will of the singer.

Throughout the melody the peculiarities of the *rāga* must appear, and unrecognized variations are not allowed, except in those cases where the Ālāp has already given notice of them. The melody is broken up into āvartas, or time sections, the number of which is usually even; and the first āvarta of each movement begins in a similar fashion.

Musical pieces in the time of the *Ratnākara* (1210-1247) were called *Prabandhas*, which name included all songs. The *Gīta Govinda* is written to *Prabandhas*, the tunes of which have now been entirely lost.

There are various kinds of melodies in use both in the north and the south. The two most important are known respectively as *Kīrtana and Kṛiti* in the south, and *Dhrupad and Khyāl* in the north. Captain Willard writes of the peculiarities of these melodies as follows:

'The melodies are short, lengthened by repetitions and variations. They all partake of the nature of what by us is called a Rondo, the piece being invariably concluded with the first strain, and sometimes with the first bar, or at least with the first note of the bar. A bar, or a measure, or a certain number of measures are frequently repeated with slight variations almost *ad libitum*. There is as much liberty allowed with respect to pauses, which may be lengthened at pleasure, provided the time is not disturbed.'

These melodies consist of a number of parts. In the south these are called *Pallavi*, *Anupallavi* and *Charaṇam*; and in the north, *Astāī*, *Antarā*, *Sañchārī* and *Ābhog*. The *Pallavi* or the *Astāī* contains the main subject of the melody focussed on the aṁśa. The *Anupallavi* or the *Antarā* contains the second subject focussed on the saṁvādī, and usually includes notes of the higher tetrachord. The *Charaṇam* or *Sañchārī* contains phrases from both the former, with or without modifications. The melody finally returns to the *Pallavi* or the *Astāī*, and closes on it or on its first phrase. Sometimes the *Charaṇam* in South Indian music is formed from the *Pallavi* and *Anupallavi* together. The *Pallavi* is sometimes translated 'chorus', and it does play the part of a chorus to the *Kīrtana*. Sometimes the *Anupallavi* is omitted, and the song only contains *Pallavi* and *Charaṇam*. In northern music we have also what is called the Ābhog, which is really a Coda, and often includes the name of the composer. *Kīrtanas* are sometimes called *Varṇa*. The difference between *Kīrtana* and *Kṛiti* is that the parts of the latter are not so distinct from one another as are the parts of the former. Not only so, but in *Kṛitis* any number of variations or Saṅgatis are allowed. Sometimes there will be as many as twelve different varieties of the same Pallavi.

Tyāgarāja greatly improved the Kṛiti. He was very fond of this style and most of his songs are Kṛitis. In some of them he is said to have exhausted every possible manner of combining the different notes of the *rāga*. These alaṅkāra (ornaments) usually occur either at the beginning or at the end of an āvarta.

The same is true to a certain extent of the Dhrupad and the Khyāl. The former are almost entirely without ornament, while the latter are allowed to use all kinds, and freely make use of them. The Dhrupad is a solemn religious song, while the Khyāl is a light melodic air.

The *Dhrupad* is usually in slow time and in selected tālas such as Āditāla, Rūpaka tāla, Chautāla, and Dhīma tāla. Dhrupad singing was introduced by Rajah Mān Singh of Gwalior (c. 1470). It is very exacting, demanding a voice of the large compass of about three octaves. 'The man who has the strength of five buffaloes, let that man sing Dhrupad,' runs an old saying. Tān Sen was a great Dhrupad singer, and Rāmpur is the home to-day of some of his celebrated descendants, who are experts at this style of singing.

Seshanna—a celebrated vīṇā player of Mysore

A kālakshepa party

Group of parayas with horns and drums

The *Sādras* is a kind of fast Dhrupad, sung in Jhampa tāla.

The *Khyāl* was introduced later than the Dhrupad, in order to find a place for the graces which are not allowed in the former. It was introduced by Amīr Khusrū and Sultan Husain, and developed by Sādarāṅga in the time of Sultan-Alāu-d-din (1296—1316). It is very similar to the Kṛiti of the south. It is usually a love song and is supposed to be sung by a woman. Khyāl singers and Dhrupad singers are usually different. The latter consider the Khyāl style to be too unclassical for them to use at all. The Khyāl singer belongs to the class called Kavvāl singers.

The *Hori* are songs descriptive of the Holi festival in December–January, and are sung by Dhrupad singers. They also have Astāī, Antarā, Sañchārī and Ābhog. They are usually sung in Dhamār tāla (5-5-4), but Khyāl singers also sing them in Dīpachandī tāla (3-4-3-4).

The *Thumri* is a love song in Hindusthani music. The music is lively and is well adapted to pantomine or dancing. It mixes up different *rāgas* and so is somewhat looked down upon by high class musicians, and it also makes use of common *rāgas* called Dhuns. Some of these tunes are very fascinating; indeed it was one of these simple little melodies that kept a whole company of musical experts enraptured at Delhi during one of the sessions of the All-India Music Conference.

The *Tappā* is the typical Muhammadan song. It has been taken up in the south also, where it is called *Hindusthani Tappā.* It gives full opportunity for the exhibition of all the graces so essential to Indian music. The melody is so rich in these as almost to be overloaded with them. All these songs have a very marked rhythm and are usually in madhya kāla. *Tappā* songs consist as a rule of two movements only, Astāī and Antarā. It is said to be similar to an ancient style of singing mentioned in the *Ratnākara* and called Visāragīti. The Tappā style of singing was first introduced by the famous singer, Shouri of Lucknow (c. 1810). It is usually set to a love song, and is very common in Hindī and Punjābī.

The *Ghazal* and the *Dādrā* are two other Hindusthani melodies. They consist as a rule of Antarā only, sung alike to a simple melody in syncopated time, which is known as Pashto (see page 76). The *Ghazals* are usually love lyrics. The Christian Church has made a large use of Hindusthani Ghazals in its hymnology.

The *Mārsīya* are songs describing the battle in which the grandsons of the Prophet were killed. They are sung in the mornings during the days of the Moharram festival. The *rāgas* used in them are mixed, and the words are chanted in a kind of recitative.

Sargam or *Svarāvarta* or *Svarasāhityā* or *Svaramālikā* are sol-fa passages or complete songs in sol-fa, in which the Indian sol-fa initials take the place of words. The word Sargam comes from the first four sol-fa initials combined, viz. **Sa Ri Ga Ma**, omitting the vowels of **Ri Ma**. This solmization is very common throughout India in both northern and southern music, and is considered quite a thing to be cultivated even by the best musicians. It is also a common thing to hear children, who know nothing about music, singing these syllables to different notes of the scale. Even the greatest musicians make use of this device in their songs. It is found frequently in Tyāgarāja.

The *Tarāna* or *Tillāna* is a similar melody making use of drum or tāla syllables instead of the sol-fa syllables. They use such syllables as taka taka tadingina tōm, tillālai lai lō, tānana nānana, etc. The Tillāla song, as it is called, is very often heard from the bullock-cart driver, as he slowly wends his way along the dusty road. Sometimes these drum or tāla mnemonics occur just as a kind of chorus. These songs are exceedingly popular and may be compared with the song Tārārāboomdeay and its like.

There is also a kind of song called *Trivata*, which consists of nonsense words extemporized by the singer. It is a song beloved of boatmen and dhooly bearers, as they take the sahib to his destination. Every alternate line is some improvisation telling of the sahib's supposed generosity, followed by a line of meaningless jingle. Or the whole thing may be a meaningless collection of mere words

The *Chaturaṅga* (four sections) is a song consisting of Khyāl, Tarāna, Sargam and Trivata.

The *Rāgamālikā* or *Rāgmālā* consists of a series of *rāgas* all linked together into one composition. Only a few phrases from each *rāga* will be given. The whole must not simply be a string of melodies, but must have a unity. The word means 'a garland of *rāgas*' and aptly describes the composition. One southern example of this form runs as follows. First of all, in six different verses come melodies in the *rāgas Śrī, Ārabhī, Gaurī, Nāṭa, Gauḍa, Mohana,* one for each verse. Then follows one verse of six lines which combines them all, one in each line. After this comes another eight *rāgas* in eight separate verses, and then another verse of eight lines, which takes them up in the inverse order in the different lines.

The *Bhajana* is a favourite form of religious musical recital, in which a choir sings after a leader, accompanied by an orchestra. The subject of a *Bhajana* may be a story from the *Rāmāyaṇa* or the *Mahābhārata,* or it may consist of songs taken at random from the devotional poets.

The *Harikathā* or *Kālakshepa* is somewhat similar to this, except that often there is no choir at all, and the singer is just accompanied by a small orchestra, while he expounds his subject in song. This is the favourite method of religious exposition in India, and has been very largely adopted by Christian evangelists in South India during recent years.

In Bengal the *Kīrtan* is somewhat similar to this, with peculiarities all its own. The Kīrtan in Bengal is a kind of dramatic sonata, which was first introduced at the time of Chaitanya in connection with the Bhakti revival. The theme develops from phase to phase and from emotion to emotion, and is generally based on a distinct part of the Kṛishṇa legend. It gives plenty of scope for originality and improvisation. The *rāga* also changes with the emotion, and both music and melody are fluid and not rigidly bound to definite modes. There is usually a choir to help the leader, and a small orchestra. In the Marāṭhā country, the name *Kīrtan* is usually given to a *Bhajana* performance.

Abhangas and *Ovis* are songs peculiar to Marāṭhī. The former are simple religious songs in any *rāga*, and were cultivated by Tukārām and the other bhakti leaders of the Marāṭhā land. N. V. Tilak, a Christian poet, often called the poet-laureate of western India, has composed many of these on patriotic and Christian subjects, which are very popular both among Christians and others. The *Ovis* is a style of song used for long epics.

Povāda are Marāṭhā, and *Karkhās* Rājput war-songs. These fighting races of Western and Central India have made much of this war music. They are about the only peoples in India who have any distinctive war-songs.

Javādis are songs sung by Kanarese singers and consist only of *Charaṇam*.

In addition to all the regular musical forms mentioned above, there are also a number of folk songs set in other modes which have come down from time immemorial, most of them having a very fascinating lilt and rhythm. In Bengal these are called *Baul* songs. In South India they are known as *Sindhu* songs, such as *Kāvadi Sindhu*, 'the songs of the pilgrims carrying their little decorated yokes' to the great temples; *Noṇḍi Sindhu*, the halting Sindhu with its hopping-like rhythm; *Tenmāngu*, the songs of the harvesters and the cartmen. Many of these are in some kind of syncopated time, which seems to come so natural to the Indian villager.

The *Nāṭakas* (dramas) of India provide a feast for the music-lover. These are usually operatic throughout, and the managers make it their study to get hold of the best airs that exist. One can hear Indian music in some of its best phases in these dramas. The music of course is mostly popular and does not reach the high classical standard of the great singers, but since that is so often associated with a rigid adherence to certain forms and technicalities, difficult of appreciation by the common man and by the foreigner, it is possible to find in this dramatic music a charm and a sweetness unaffected by technicalities, hard for the uninitiated to appreciate. Among the most popular of these song-dramas are the stories of King Harischandra, King Nala, Sāvitrī, the various episodes in the life of Rāma and Sītā, and stories of the saints of the bhakti revival. The large towns have many dramatic companies which give regular performances, and strolling troupes of varying ability wander through the country and perform in the villages from time to time, so that every villager in India knows these dramas almost as well or even better than the townsman. As a matter of fact, it is a custom in many villages for the people themselves to get up their own dramas, in which certain classes, usually from the lower castes, provide the actors by ancient right and custom. It is therefore quite common to find some of the best singers in these classes.

The *Saṅkīrtan* and the *Nagarkīrtan* are popular musical performances, usually of a religious character. They have been most highly developed in Bengal. The meaning of Saṅkīrtan is 'united praise', and it denotes a large choir who sit on the floor and sing to the accompaniment of instruments. *Nagarkīrtan* is used of a procession of devotees who go through the streets of a city, singing and dancing to musical accompaniments, and carrying many banners.

The Drone. All Indian music is played or sung to a drone. This takes the place of harmony in providing the background for the melody. Without the drone, the singer would feel as 'a ship without a rudder.' The drone consolidates the melody as well as provides the background. When other instruments are quiet it keeps on the sound, so that the singer can pick up the music again, without any chance of pitching on the wrong note. There are of course songs without the drone, like that of the cartman on his lonely journey, the boatman on the backwater, the mother to her child; but in all public musical entertainments a drone of some kind is essential. The drone may be supplied by the drum only, the keynote and the Pañchama of the two heads respectively giving all that is absolutely necessary. As a rule, however, it is the custom to have another instrument for the drone. The best instrument for this purpose is the Tambūr. This gives the tonic, the fifth and sometimes the fourth, and makes a most charming background for the melody. The custom has come in recently to use the harmonium for the drone. This is undoubtedly convenient, but the noise is not by any means attractive, nor likely to add to the appreciation of Indian music by ears trained to quality as well as to pitch. There is also a special wind instrument called the *Drone* which is used for this purpose with flutes and reeds. The vīṇā, sitār, sāraṅgī, dilrūba and many other stringed instruments have their own drone-strings, which are struck more or less regularly as the melody is being played. The drone, as may be supposed, goes on throughout the whole performance without cessation, but strange to relate does not tend to monotony, as one might think. It helps to bring out the variety of the melody built above it. The sāraṅgī and the sitār have, in addition, a number of sympathetic strings, from sixteen to twenty-two, placed below the main strings and never played on, which give out a very attractive humming sound all the time the instrument is played, and provide a kind of re-inforced drone to the whole music.

Only a few of the melodies of India are described above. India is the land of melody. In such a great continent of so many races it is only natural to find some more musical than others Stopping one evening in a Bengal village we heard on every side of us different kinds of music. There was nothing discordant and it all blended together into a pleasing harmony. Our boat had drawn up by a small landing stage, while the boatmen went to their food. Out in the stream were other boats, their occupants singing love lyrics or devotional songs, as they rested for a time after their meal. In one boat was a musical party with tambūr and drum. As we strolled round the village, we heard from house after house the sounds of melody. Here a woman was singing to her baby. There a man was chanting the story of some ancient hero. In another house we heard the esrāj, the Bengālī sāraṅgī, being played. In another a Muhammadan was playing the harmonium and singing to the music. The voices were sweet and composed, and the melodies were as a rule simple melodies that the village people loved. I can remember another evening in the Marāṭhā country on the hill top of Matherān near Bombay, going out into the glorious moonlight to listen to the song of two women as they ground their corn. One of them would sing a line telling of some deed of Kṛishṇa, and then there would be silence, broken only by the sound of the two grinding stones rolling one on top of the other. Then the other would take up the song and carry on the story. Then silence again, or rather the musical silence of the grinding, which was as the drone note to the melody. Then again the song went on, and so on, until suddenly they discovered we were listening, and the melody stopped for that night, and all that we heard was the dull grinding sound, which still seemed to carry with it memories of that song of haunting sweetness, sung by the limpid voices of those women. I can remember another night on the back-waters of Travancore in the extreme south-west of India. I was in a boat such as was used in the olden days by the chiefs of that land. The boat had been lent by the Metropolitan of the ancient Syrian Christian Church and was manned by twelve stalwart rowers. All night long they sang their ancient songs, strange melodies, sometimes with nonsense words, sometimes about trees and hills and forests, sometimes about the Virgin Mary, for they were Catholics, and all with some ending suggestive of the oarsman's pull, which seemed every time to help forward the boat. The ending was something like this, Tīya Tīya—Teya Teya, with an emphasis on the first syllable of each beat, marking the pull of the oar. I slept off and on as we passed under the lovely palms through the moonlight, puzzling my brain as to how they found breath for steady rowing and continual singing. I remember another evening sitting in a lonely bungalow far away from all towns, with a little village near by. The day had been hot and dusty and it was some Hindu festival. Just close by was a little village shrine to the god Subramaniyar, the warlike son of Śiva. After dinner was over I heard the sound of singing coming from this temple, and going out, found two young men from the village learning the old devotional songs from a temple musician. He would sing a line, and then they would take it up after him. They were simple melodies set to beautiful words of devotion, but in that quiet village they made one feel the beating heart of India.

Another time while I was staying for a few days in the realm of His Highness the Nawāb of Rāmpur, descendant of a celebrated musical house, I heard some of the classical music of northern India played and sung by its famous musicians. Here are still descendants of the celebrated Tān Sen, the most wonderful singer of the days of the Muhammadan Empire, and his musical tradition is alive in the court. His Highness the Nawāb himself is an expert singer of Dhrupads, composed by the great Mīyān Tān Sen, and Sāhabzada Sādat Ali Khān Bahadur, the Home Secretary of the State, has found time to give to the cultivation of music. He himself is one of the very few expert players on the old rabāb, the instrument played by Tān Sen, and the precursor of the modern Sur-ṣṛingāra. With its wide bowl and metalled finger-board and its scope for all the peculiar slides and shakes of Hindusthani music, it sent forth under the hands of its skilled player now deep full sounds, and now the sweet high-toned metallic sounds of a metal string. Then came a famous Dhrupad singer. He started with an Ālāp bringing out, one after the other, with fine full voice, the central notes and phrases of the *rāga*. It was the *Hindol rāga* with its sharpened **Ma** and with a glorious slide from the **Ga** to the **Sa**. He sang a solemn song, each note full and clear, with none of the lilts and graces which we are wont to associate with Indian singing, and occasionally using the full ascent and descent of the scale to show all its peculiarities, as well as the power and fulness of the singer's voice. There was no nasal tone here, but all from the chest. Some years back I heard a woman weeping for her husband, who had died the day before. She was a Paraya woman, one of the lowest classes in the southern peninsula, but she sang out her grief in sad and haunting recitative, the music set to words of poignant sorrow.

'What shall I look at so as to forget. No longer do I see him. He has gone and left me. What was it mine enemv said ? Now begins the burning. My very blood has dried up.'

As she sang she beat her breasts, pacing up and down in front of the poor little hut of thatch and mud in the centre of the outcaste village, which was her home. Then away to the north in the great wheat-plains of the Punjab, as the women harvest the crops of wheat which go to feed the millions of North India and also the people of England, singers and dhol drummers are hired, so that the women may keep pace with the music and get through their task in the quickest possible time. All day long the songs go on: primitive Punjābī folk-tunes, and in some Christian villages the Psalms as set to these old tunes by the early missionaries.

So wherever one goes in India one finds music interwoven with life and playing its part in the culture and business of every day.

CHAPTER VII

THE MUSICAL INSTRUMENTS OF INDIA

THE musical instruments of India present a wonderful variety. As might be expected they are meant mostly for individual use, and there is very little suggestion of an orchestra. The Indian Rājas maintain a number of fine musicians, but it is rare to hear orchestral music in India. It is not, however, unknown, and one may sometimes hear orchestral pieces at the concerts of the Gāndharva Mahāvidyālaya in Bombay and also in Baroda. In order to see all the different musical instruments of India one has to journey to many different places. There is a good collection at the Gāndharva Mahāvidyālaya in Bombay; but the Indian Museum, Calcutta, has probably the finest collection of both ancient and modern instruments. One does not however, as a rule, find them in a band or concert party, as one does in the West, though Baroda is attempting to do this under the guidance of Mr. Fredilis, the Principal of the Music School and an accomplished western musician. The greatest variety is found in stringed instruments and in instruments of percussion. Probably India excels most other countries in these two. The following quotation from the monumental work by Captain Day on *The Musical Instruments of Southern India* will give a good idea of the condition of things when he wrote fifty years ago:—

'Most of the early musical instruments remain still in use. Since the time of the Muhammadan invasion, about a thousand years ago, some Arabian and Persian instruments have been adopted, and have become almost naturalized; but their use has never become universal, and is mostly confined to the North of India or to Mussulman musicians.

'The people of India have always been conservative in their tastes, and in nothing do we find this more evident than in their music and musical instruments. Descriptions of them are found in many of the old Sanskrit treatises, and show that the forms of the instruments now in use have altered hardly at all during the last two thousand

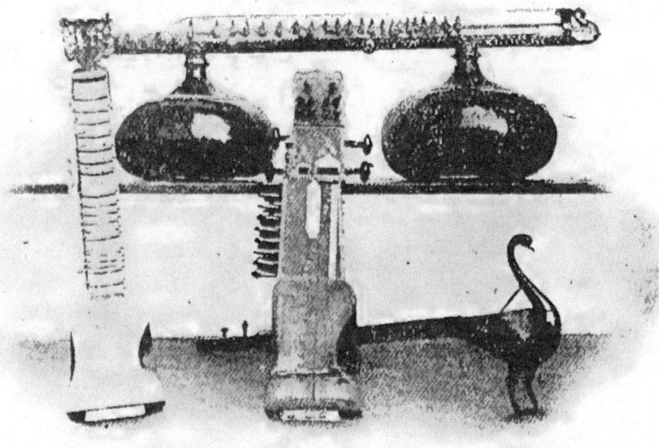

Group of stringed instruments (northern)

Bīṇ

Dilruba Sāraṅgī Peacock sitār

Some ancient instruments

Svaramaṇḍala Brahmā vīṇā

Kuṛal Bastran

Vīṇā Sitār Tambūr

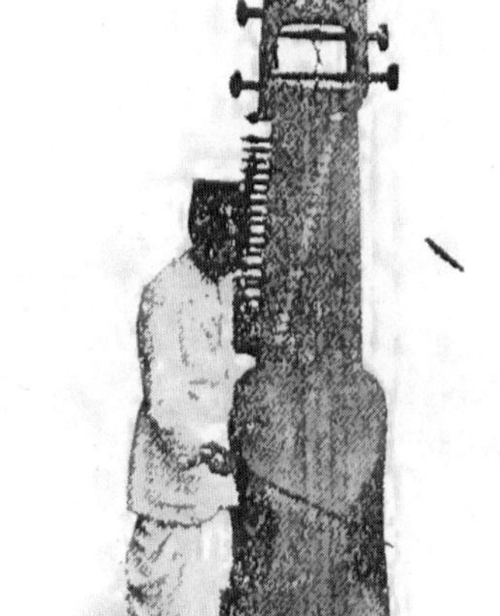

An orchestral sāraṅgī

Playing various stringed instruments

years; old paintings and sculptures, such as those of Ajanta, prove this even more conclusively. There are many musical instruments to be found among the sculptures existing upon various old cave-temples and ancient Buddhist topes and stupas in different parts of India.

'Those at Amrāvatī and Sāñchī are especially interesting. For in the Amrāvatī sculptures, which were visited by the traveller, Hiouen Thsang, and called by him Dhananacheka, about the year 640 of our era, we find several representations of musical instruments. One of peculiar interest shows a group of eighteen women playing upon drums, a shell trumpet or *śaṅkha*, one much like a *surnāī*, and two instruments, apparently *quanūns*, of a shape very similar to the Assyrian harps. But there is another instrument represented that would seem to have been especially popular, but which is never met with in India now, nor can descriptions of it be found in the Sanskrit treatises upon instruments. This again figures in Assyrian and Egyptian sculptures and paintings. It is somewhat like a harp, and much like an African instrument called Sancho, still used in some parts of that continent.

'This peculiar harp is again found amongst the sculptures at Sāñchī; where also is seen an instrument resembling the Roman tibae pares. But the tibae pares are there shown without the capistrum or cheek bandage, and it is known that this instrument was also used by the Greeks. It is worthy of note that a form of the tibae pares is still common in northern India, where it consists of a pair of flutes. At Sāñchī too is found a figure of a man blowing a kind of trumpet—the śṛiṅga—of much the same shape as that now employed in Bengal.

The materials of which musical instruments are made are for the most part those that are found readiest to hand in the country. Bamboo or some similar cane and large gourds are much employed. These gourds are used for many purposes, and the best are trained in their growth to the shape for which they are required.

'In the manufacture of certain instruments earthenware is employed; the common country blackwood is largely used; in fact, whatever is found by the instrument makers, that from its natural shape, or the ease with which it can be worked, can be adapted with the least possible trouble to themselves, is readily seized upon, whether its acoustical properties are suitable or not, purity of tone being sacrificed to appearance. The natural consequence of this is that many instruments are badly put together in the first place; faults in their construction are glossed over by outward ornamentation, and from want of proper material, the tone, which should be the first consideration, is frequently sadly deficient in volume and quality.

'The Persians still use an instrument called *quanūn*, much like that of the same name found in India—a kind of dulcimer strung with gut or wire strings, and played upon by plectra fastened to the fingers of the performers. That is a development of the *Kattyāyana-vīṇā* or *śatatantrī* (hundred stringed) *vīṇā*, as it was formerly called. The Persian *quanūn*, the prototype of the mediaeval psaltery, afterwards became the santir, which has strings of wire instead of gut, and is played with two sticks; and in the west it actually took the form of the dulcimer. Hence the origin of the complicated pianoforte of the present day can thus be traced to the Aryans. And so with many others. The violin, the flute, the oboe, the guitar, all have an Eastern origin. One of the earliest of stringed instruments was called "*Pinaka,*" and had one string twanged by the fingers; its invention is ascribed to the god Śiva. The violin bow is claimed by the Hindus to have been invented by Rāvaṇa, King of Lanka (Ceylon), who according to tradition lived more than five thousand years ago.

'The earliest instrument played with a bow was called *Rabanastra* or *Rabanastrana*. What this instrument was like is rather doubtful; but at the present time there exists in Ceylon a primitive instrument played with a bow, called "*Vinavah*", which has two strings of different kinds; one made of a species of flax, and the other of horse-hair, which is the material also of the string of the bow, which with bells attached to it is used as a fiddle stick. The hollow part of this instrument is half a cocoanut shell polished, covered with a dried skin of a lizard and perforated below.'

The *Vinavah* is mentioned in the classical books and the name suggests an instrument made of bamboo. It is rarely met with except in the hands of strolling musicians, who support themselves by means of it. Whether this is the primitive *rabanastra* or not it is impossible to say; but it seems extremely probable that, if not absolutely identical, it bears at least a very strong resemblance to it. Another very ancient instrument which resembled the *Rabanastra* was called *Amṛita.*

Numbers of instruments still in use in India have not altered in the smallest particular their ancient forms. The *Vīṇā*, the *Tambūr* or *Tambūrī-vīṇā*, and the *Kinnarī* still remain just as they are described in the ancient books, even down to the very details of the carving with which they are adorned, so conservative are the people who use them of all connected with the art they hold to be so sacred.

The peculiar shape of instruments of the viola and violin tribe appears to have a prototype among Indian instruments; and this can be seen in the *Rabāb*, which is made with distinct upper, lower and middle bouts, and in a lesser degree in the *Sāraṅgī*, *Sāroda*, and *Chikāra*. The rebec once popular in Europe was a form of the rabāb, brought to Spain by the Moors, who in turn had derived it from Persia and Arabia. Here again the Aryan origin is evident, the rabāb being, according to old Sanskrit works, a form of vīṇā. And it is still popular in the North of India and Afghanistan.

The use of instruments of percussion of definite sonorousness, such as the harmonica, does not seem to have entered into Indian music at any time until quite of late years. But this is rather an open question, for the harmonicon of cups, called *Jalatarangiṇī*, is by some ascribed to a very remote origin.

Wind instruments, although perhaps of earlier invention than those with strings, are nevertheless looked upon as of secondary importance. Possibly this may have some reason in the fact that Brahmans are not allowed by their religious laws to use them, excepting the flute blown by the nostrils, and one or two others of the horn and trumpet kind. And so men of low castes are employed as players of wind instruments. But all unite in ascribing to wind instruments a very high antiquity. The conch shell, still used in the daily temple ritual in almost every place in India, is said to have been first used by the god Krishṇa, and it is mentioned in the great epic of the *Rāmāyaṇa*, where it is called Devadatta.[1] We also find it under the name of Gośriṅga, both in the *Rāmāyaṇa* and the *Mahābhārata*.

The horn (*śriṅga*) is also said to be of divine origin, and it is mentioned in the earliest writings. But the flute (*muralī*) is still held to be peculiarly sacred, for this flute was the companion of the god Krishna in all his wanderings; and in Indian mythology, this flute is looked upon with much the same veneration that the lyre was by the Greeks, and even by Brahmans it is still occasionally played and blown by the nostrils. In all sculptures and pictures, the god Krishna is represented as standing cross-legged playing the flute.

Reed instruments, although doubtless of very remote origin, appear to have been invented at a later period than instruments of the flute species, and their use is usually confined to either low caste Hindus or Mohammadans. For the Indian reed instruments are mostly harsh and wild, far too powerful and shrill to be used in concert with the delicate vīṇā or sweet tambūr, and so their use is chiefly confined to out-of-door performances, where their sound is better heard and where they become fit adjuncts to the band. Instruments with double reeds appear to have been originally brought from India, and the double reed is found in the primitive oboes used there as well as in Persia, Arabia and Egypt. There seems to be no trace of the single beating reed ever having been known in India, but the single free reed is found in the bagpipe of the country. Indeed the bagpipe would itself seem to have an Eastern origin; and, although its use in Southern India and the Deccan is chiefly confined to a drone-bass, yet in the Punjab and Afghanistan pipes are sometimes found containing both drone and chanter. I have heard them played with a dexterity that would do credit to a Highland piper. The *Puṅji*, now used almost entirely by snake-charmers, is said to have once been blown by the nostrils and called Nāsajantra.—(Captain Day. 99–104.)

Captain Day's remarks on instrument-making are not so applicable to-day as they were when he wrote fifty years ago. There is a constantly increasing demand for musical instruments, and a class of instrument-makers is arising. The centres of this industry are found in Calcutta, Miraj

[1] i.e., god-given.

and Tanjore; and many of the makers are noted for their skill, and the resonant qualities of instruments are being looked to very much more. The public is also taking up with zest the question of musical education, and it is becoming frequent in the better-class families to arrange for their daughters to learn some Indian instrument. All this, with the revived interest in music, will mean, as time goes on, a development of skill in the proper construction of instruments such as Captain Day desires. The Chitpur Road, Calcutta, is the centre of instrument-making in Bengal.

Captain Day in his book mentions the bells which are a common feature of festival dances in India, though hardly to be classed as musical instruments. They are usually tied round the ankles of the dancers. They are also used on festival occasions for the bulls. Every post-runner in India has a few attached to his little spear, and these may be heard for a very long distance as the runner comes along to the village.

I. Stringed Instruments

Apart from the drum the largest variety of musical instruments in India is found among the strings. The best and the most honourable instruments are also found here. The *Vīṇā* occupies the first place among them all, and has done so from time immemorial. It is also the instrument par excellence for rendering Indian music; and no one who has not heard the masters of the vīṇā has any right to give a final judgment on Indian music. In northern India the vīṇā is often called *Bīn*, the name vīṇā being given to the tambūr. In this book, however, the name vīṇā is consistently used for the classical instrument of that name. Three places in India are noted for its manufacture. They are Tanjore and Mysore in South India, and Miraj in Western India. The Tanjore and Mysore makes differ in the wood used for the bowl. Tanjore uses jackwood and Mysore blackwood. Nearly all Tanjore vīṇās are elaborately ornamented by ivory carvings.

The instrument consists of a large pea-shaped bowl

hollowed out of one piece of wood, either jackwood or blackwood. The flat top of this bowl is about one foot in diameter. The bridge is placed on the bowl, and near it are a number of small sound-holes. The construction of the bridge is peculiar.

'A wooden arc supports a slab of wood, one inch by two and a half inches. A resinal cement is poured upon this and a piece of metal, passing underneath the second, third and fourth strings, is laid above and manipulated until the strings produce a clear tone free from all buzz or twang; a wet cloth is then applied, or a little cold water poured over the upper surface, so as to harden the cement. Under the first string a similar piece of metal, in this case of superior quality, either polished steel or bell-metal, is fixed in the same way. This process is considered very important, as the least carelessness affects the tone of the instrument and gives it a most unpleasant twang.'—(Captain Day.)

The side-string bridge is secured to the main bridge and the belly of the instrument, and is made entirely of metal. It consists of an arc of brass, with a projecting rim upon the side nearest the attachment. The body of the instrument is made of the same kind of wood as the belly, and is hollowed out thin. A projecting ledge of ivory separates the body from the stem. The neck is attached to the body also with ivory, and is usually curved downward into some weird figure. This also is hollow. Into the body just beyond the neck is fixed a hollow gourd on the under side, which forms a kind of rest for the vīṇā and is useful also to increase the volume of the sound. This gourd is easily detachable. The frets of the instrument are made of brass or silver, and are secured to two ledges running along each side of the stem of the instrument. These ledges are made of some wax-like substance which can be softened by gentle heat, so that the position of the frets can be changed, if desired. There are altogether twenty-four frets, so that each string contains two complete octaves. Many Indian scholars are of opinion that the ancient books give no ground for thinking that any of the old classical musicians used more than twelve frets for the octave on the vīṇā. The tuning-pegs to the main frets are fixed two in each side of the neck, and the strings pass over the ivory bridge between the neck and the stem.

The three pegs for the side strings are fixed in the side of the stem just above the gourd.

The vīṇā has seven strings, four of which pass over the frets and constitute the main playing strings, and the other three of which are placed at the side of the finger-board, and are used to play a kind of drone accompaniment to the melody and to mark the time.

The two thinnest strings, which are on the side nearest the player, are of steel, and the other two main strings are of brass or silver. The three side strings are of steel. Each string has a distinct name, which are, beginning from the thinnest, Sāraṇī, Pañchama, Mandaran, Anumandaran. The three side strings are called Pakka-Sāraṇī, and sometimes Chikāri, a name common to all such side strings.

There are various ways of tuning the instrument. The following are said to be those generally accepted, beginning from the playing strings :—

Main Strings. Side Strings.

(*a*) Sa Pa Sa Sa (C G C C) Pa Sa Pa (G C G_1)
(*b*) Pa Sa Pa Pa (G C G_1 G_1) Sa Pa Sa (C G_1 C_1)
(*c*) Ma Ṣa Pa Sa (F C G_1 C_1) Sa Sa Pa (C^1 C G)

One at Rampur I noted was tuned thus:

(*d*) Ma Sa Pa Ga (F C G_1 E_1) Sa Sa Pa or Ni or Sa (C^1 C^1 G or B or C)

(*e*) Captain Day notes one at Miraj tuned thus: It only had two side strings.

Ma Sa Pa Sa (F C G_1, C_1), Sa Sa (C C_1)

(*c*) and (*d*) are the common ways of tuning in upper India.

The first two strings are always the ones played upon most, though expert players will use all of them easily.

The frets of the vīṇā are placed in different positions on different instruments. The tendency in South India to-day is to use the intervals of equal temperament. Mr. Ellis mentions testing a vīṇā many years ago in the South and finding the intervals those of equal temperament. Captain Day mentions an old Tanjore vīṇā whose frets were placed at intervals, which were found to be slightly flatter than the notes of the tempered scale.

The vīṇā may be held either in a horizontal position across the player's knees or else slanting against the shoulder. Different players have different styles. The

Mayūri

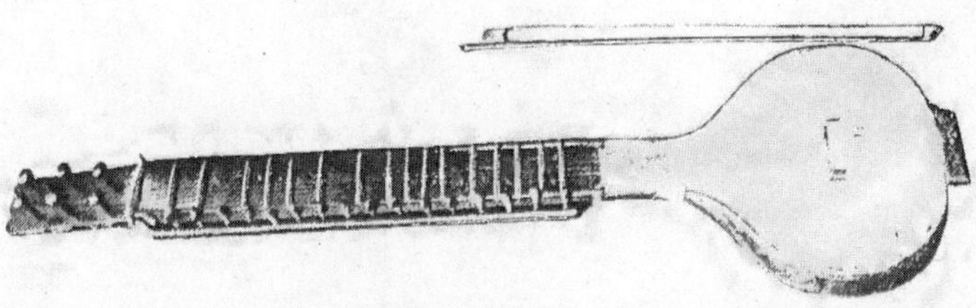

Esrāj

Vīṇā (Southern)

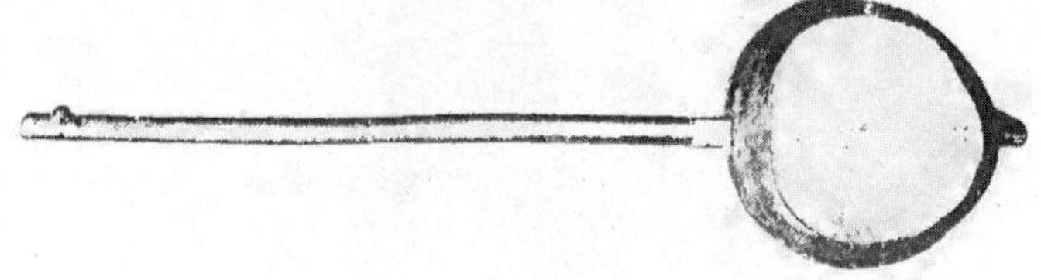

Ektār

Stringed instruments

Vīṇā Sitār Tambur

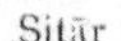

An orchestral sāraṅgī

Playing various stringed instruments

pictures in this chapter give specimens of each style. It is played by the right hand, the left hand passing round the stem and stopping the strings.

The vīṇā is played either with the finger nails or with a plectrum. The finest players use their finger nails; but many amateurs, who do not wish to grow the nails long, have taken to the plectrum. In South India it is quite common to find amateurs playing the vīṇā, and it is becoming increasingly the thing for girls to learn it. In the north, however, it is usually only professionals who play it. The instruments for amateurs in the north are the sitār and the esrāj, or dilruba. The main strings of the vīṇā are played with the first three fingers, the fourth finger being used for the side strings, just striking them at intervals, in time with the tāla used. The main strings are stopped between the frets, but the side strings are always open. The vīṇā lends itself to all the different graces which give so much beauty to Indian music, and in the hands of really capable performers it produces most wonderful and charming effects. It is an ideal instrument for an Indian girl to learn. It is hoped that more and more the unsuitable harmonium, with its strident tones, will give place to this beautiful Indian instrument, an instrument affording not only delight to player and hearers, but also real culture.

There are different kinds of vīṇā called after the shape of the head, such as the Peacock vīṇā, Rudra vīṇā.

The *Sitār* is perhaps the most common instrument in North India. It is not yet found much in the south, but there is little doubt that, as Indian music is cultivated more and more, this simple and beautiful instrument will come very largely into use all over the south. It is well suited either for the amateur or the professional. It is not difficult for the amateur to learn to play simple melodies upon it, and at the same time it lends itself to all the subtle arts of the professional, whereby he can show his skill or the charm of the music. The principles of the sitār are the same as those of the vīṇā, but there are considerable differences in construction. It is a much smaller instrument and is more easily carried about. Like the vīṇā it has a belly made of jack or some other resonant wood, but there is no curved neck and no gourd. The body of the instrument is about two feet long, and carries the finger-board, which is about three inches wide. The bowl is from eight inches to one foot in width. The bridge is placed on the bowl, but is not double as in the vīṇā. The strings pass over this, and then over another ledge beyond the frets, and again through holes in a ledge near the pegs. These ledges are usually made of ivory. All the strings are over the finger-board. The tuning-pegs are placed, four on the face of the instrument at the end and three at the side, at varying distances from the end. The number of strings is usually seven. The frets are curved and are made of metal, usually brass, and they are fixed by means of wire strings tied round the body of the instrument. They are movable at the will of the player. It is therefore easy to alter the tune of the sitār or the size of any particular intervals. The frets vary from sixteen to eighteen in number for about an octave and a half on each string. The Carnatic sitār is somewhat different. It has a much thinner and shorter neck and is shaped something like a tambūr. Only the first two strings pass over frets, which are about half an inch wide and raised from the finger-board. These two strings are placed much nearer together than the other strings. The fourth and fifth strings go round a small ivory bead about half-way up the finger-board, whence they pass obliquely under the strings to the tuning-pegs. The sixth and seventh strings pass straight up the finger-board in the usual way. All the strings except the seventh, which is of brass, are of steel. The frets are of wood with an upper edge of metal and are fixed to the finger-board. Usually there are about fourteen frets, which are placed at the intervals of the diatonic scale.

In the ordinary sitār the strings are made of steel and brass. The first, third, fifth, sixth and seventh are of steel and the other two of brass. Many sitārs have a number of sympathetic strings placed beneath the other strings, which are never played, but give a continual hum as the other strings are played.

The tuning of the strings in the ordinary sitār is usually as follows, beginning from the shortest string attached to the side peg :—

Sa Sa P̱a Pa Sa Sa Ma (C C G$_1$, G C C F)

The last string is the one usually played on, though expert players will use the last three. This string passes through a small bead at its attachment to the belly, so as to aid in tuning to the exact pitch required.

The Carnatic sitār runs thus :

Sa Pa Sa Pa Sa Sa Sa (C G C G G G C)

The instrument is played by means of a wire plectrum placed upon the forefinger of the right hand, and the strings are struck near the belly. They are stopped by pressing down the fingers of the left hand upon them right above the frets, and not just before the frets as is done on the vīṇā. As a rule, only one string is stopped, the others being used as open strings for the accompanying drone sound.

There is a beautiful sitār in the Gāndharva Mahāvidyālaya in Bombay, which has an ostrich egg for the bowl, beautifully mounted on gold. Some sitārs have peacock-shaped heads and are called Peacock sitārs. The Tarfā sitār has an extra string for the śruti or tonic. The sitār is also called *sundarī*—the beautiful.

The sitār lends itself well to the performance of Indian music, and is becoming more popular among the people generally.

The invention of the sitār is commonly credited to the famous singer Amīr Khusru of the court of Sultan Ala-u-din in the fourteenth century. It is probably of Persian origin.

The *Dilruba* is very much like a sitār, but smaller; and instead of a bowl, it has a belly, covered with sheep-parchment. In shape it is something like the sāraṅgī, and like that instrument it is played with a bow made of horse-hair. It has frets similar to the sitār, nineteen in number, which are movable. It has only the four main strings and not the extra three. The dilruba is made, as a rule, with twenty-two sympathetic strings under the main strings.

The arrangement of the tuning-pegs is like that of the four main pegs of the sitār, two being vertically on the face and two on the side. The instrument is about three feet long, and the width of the belly will be about six inches. The bow is about 1¾ feet long.

The tuning of the four strings is usually **Ṣa P̣a Sa Ma** (C1, G1, C F), the last being the principal string. The first two are brass and the last two steel. In this instrument also, the peacock shape occurs for the belly. The dilruba is not a very common instrument. It is used in the Punjab and in the United Provinces, but as a rule one sees the sāraṅgī much more frequently.

The *Surbahār* is another instrument of the sitār kind. It has a similar shape to the sitār, but the frets are not movable, and it has a finer tone and wider range. It is played with two strokes, one with the plain finger and the other a sort of mandoline tāla stroke with plectrums on the forefinger and little finger. Mr. Fox Strangways gives it the title 'dignified.' This instrument is found only in Bengal. It lends itself very well to the graces of Indian music.

The *Sāraṅgī* is the Indian violin. It is shaped, however, something like a small guitar. The instrument is made from one block of wood hollowed out, and it has a parchment-covered belly. It is smaller than the sitār, being as a rule about two feet in height. The sāraṅgī may have either three or four strings, three being gut and one brass. The brass string is the lowest in pitch. The bridge is fixed in the middle of the belly, with a support under the parchment. The instrument is played usually with a bow, but sometimes a plectrum is used. The four tuning-pegs are fixed at each side of the head, which is hollow. The tuning of the four strings is as follows, in accordance with the *rāga*: **Sa Pa Sa, Ga** or **Ma** (C G C, E or F)

The sāraṅgī, like the western violin, has its devotees both among experts and also among the beggar fraternity. It is found throughout the north. The strings are stopped by pressing the finger against their side, and not by placing the finger upon them. This renders it possible to produce all the peculiar *gamaka* of Indian music without any

A NORTH INDIAN SARANGI PLAYER

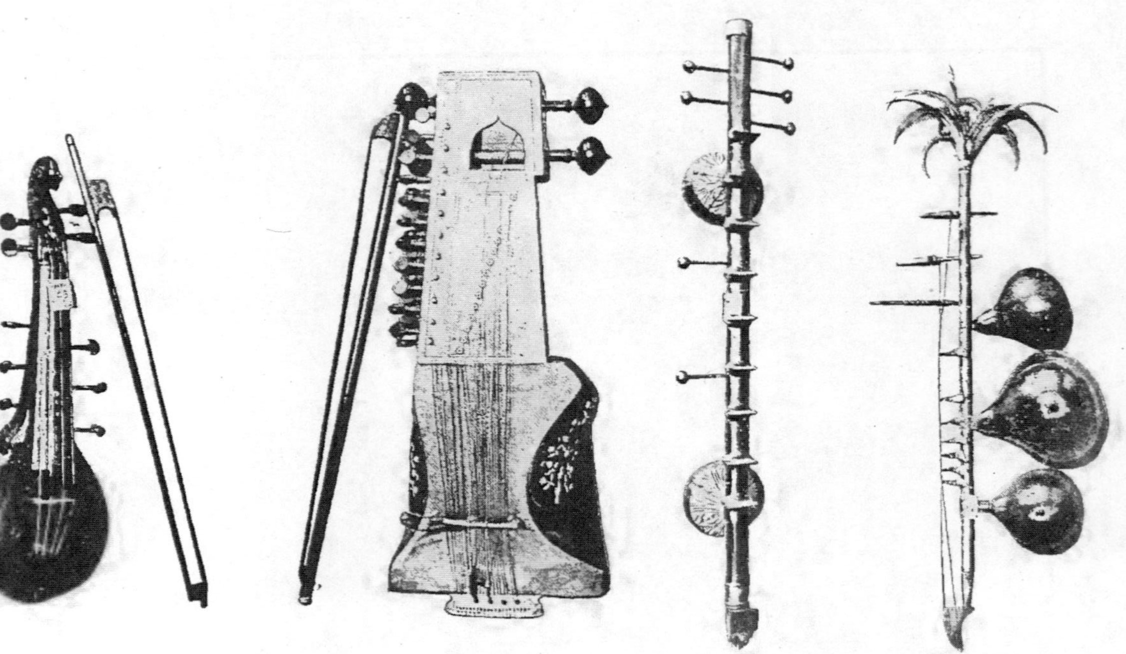

Sāraṅgī (Bengal) Sāraṅgī Mahatī Vīṇā Kinnarī

Ancient and modern stringed instruments

difficulty. The sound is mellow and somewhat resembles that of the viola. It is a very fine instrument, and expert players can get a tremendous lot from it. Even the beggar manages to produce quite a delightful noise with it. It provides a very good accompaniment for singing, and has more fulness of tone than the sitār and also very considerable possibilities of development. It seems hardly possible, however, that it will rival the violin in the power and beauty of its tone or in its range, but it will always be a good member of an Indian orchestra, and, like the viola, will come in very useful as a contrast. In the south already the violin has come to stay, and there is not much likelihood of the sāraṅgī displacing it now. It may, however, come to the south as a member of an Indian orchestra. The sāraṅgī usually has, like the other instruments already mentioned, a number of sympathetic strings, from fifteen to twenty-two, under the four main strings. The Gāndharva Mahāvidyālaya has a fine orchestral sāraṅgī which stands seven feet high, and which is meant to be used in the concerts given there, though hitherto it has been mostly ornamental. (See p. 99.)

The *Sāroda* or *Sarrawat* is a sāraṅgī played with the plectrum instead of the bow. It has a powerful tone and is usually much larger than the sāraṅgī.

The *Esrāj* is the Bengal variety of the sāraṇgī. It is a little smaller than the latter, and uses all wire strings instead of gut. The tuning is **Sa Sa Pa Ma**, (C C G F), the **Ma** string being the chief string. This is the common instrument that one finds to-day in the houses of cultured people in Bengal. It is played with a bow like the sāraṇgī.

The *Sārindā* is another variety of the sāraṇgī, peculiar to Bengal. The bottom of the instrument is oval instead of rectangular, and the upper half of the body is left open. It is played in the same way as the sārangī. It usually has an elaborate tailpiece. It has only two thin strings of gut and not four as in the sāraṇgī. It is used chiefly by jogis and fakīrs.

The *Chikāra* is a curiously shaped variety of the sāraṅgī. The body consists of a long hollow piece of wood, upon which, near the lower end, a parchment covered box is fixed. The bridge is placed upon this. It has three strings of gut or horsehair and five sympathetic strings of wire. The tuning of the three former, which are the main strings, is usually **Sa Ma Pa** (C F G) or else the same as the sāraṅgī, and that of the sympathetic strings is **Pa Dha Ni Sa Ṛi** (G A B C^1 D^1).

The *Tambūr* is perhaps the most common stringed instrument in India. It is found everywhere and its varieties are numberless. It is made both for the poor and for the rich. One sees it in the hands of the poverty-stricken beggar, and in the houses of wealthy princes. In shape it is something like the vīṇā, without the extra gourd and without the elaborate headpiece. The bowl is usually a large one about ten inches wide, and in the best kinds it is made of wood from the jack tree and hollowed out. The cheaper kinds have a gourd in place of the wooden bowl. The bridge is placed on the bowl in the centre and is made either of wood or of ivory. The strings pass through holes in a ledge placed near the pegs. The tuning-pegs of the first and second strings are fixed at the side of the neck, and those of the third and fourth strings at right-angles to the head. The strings are all of metal, three being steel and the lowest one of brass. Little pieces of silk are placed between the bridge and the strings in order to increase the buzzing effect. The strings also have beads near their attachment in order to render perfect tuning easier. The instrument is always played on the open strings by the fingers, without any plectra. The strings are never stopped. The tuning of the tambūr is as follows: **Pa Sa Sa Ṣa** (G C C C_1). The instrument is held upright with the left hand, and played by gently pulling the four strings, one after the other, from the highest to the lowest, with the fingers of the right hand. It provides a full and resonant droning accompaniment to the melody sung or played, and there is no other instrument which gives so effective a drone as this does. The effect is quite pleasing and the sound made up of the octave and fifth fits in very naturally with the music.

The best tambūr are made at Lucknow and Rāmpūr

in the north, and at Tanjore in the south; and many of them are most elaborately ornamented with ivory. No Indian orchestra is complete without the tambūr.

There is a variety of the tambūr called the *Brahmā vīṇā.* This is made like a large box and has no gourd or bowl. It is about three and a half feet long and six inches wide and stands nine inches high. There is a raised ledge in the middle, over which the strings run; and it has a fifth string at the side tuned to the higher Sa (c^1). It is used for the same purpose as the tambūr.

Sometimes players use the tambūr in quite peculiar ways. I once heard a musician play on it by stopping the strings with a small bamboo and using it more like the vīṇā. The full resonance of the tambūr and the buzzing sound gave the melody a very pleasing effect. I also heard a performer play an instrument like the tambūr by stopping it with a cocoanut. The name given to this instrument by the people is *Kōṭṭuvādyam* or *Bālaśarasvatī.* The word *koṭṭu* is said to mean 'movable fret.' It is found in a few places in South India.

The *Sursōta* is another variety of the tambūr found in the north. It has no gourd or bowl and is really a hollow trunk of bamboo. It is about three feet long and has four strings tuned similarly to the tambūr.

The *Kinnarī* is one of the primitive Indian instruments. It is supposed to have been invented by Kinnara, one of the musicians of Indra's heaven, after whom a class of musicians has been named. The instrument to-day is a beggar's instrument only. It is strange that the Bible also mentions a stringed instrument called the Kinnor, and it is possible that these may have had some connection with each other. We find the *Kinnarī* represented on many old Indian sculptures and paintings.

It is made from a piece of bamboo or blackwood, about two and a half feet long, fixed upon three gourds. There are twelve frets made of bone or metal and fixed upon the fingerboard by some resinous substance. The strings pass into a tall perpendicular peg near the last of the frets. The tailpiece of the instrument is often made to represent the tail of a kite. There are two or three strings, one of which passes over the frets, the others being the drone strings. The drone strings are tuned to the tonic and its fourth or fifth. The musical capacity of the *Kinnarī* is not great, and its sound is very weak and rather twangy.

The *Dheṅka*, found in Madras, is a similar instrument, with two cocoanuts as resonators and cowrie shells as frets.

The *Yektār* is another very primitive instrument, having, as its name implies (*Ek=one, Tār=string*), only one string. It is much used by beggars throughout India. It has an open string without any frets. It is made from a piece of bamboo, to the under side of which a large gourd or hollow cylinder of wood is attached in the same direction as the bamboo, one end being closed by a piece of parchment The string passes through a hole in the centre of the parchment. It is about three or four feet long. This instrument is the beggar's band and gives a twanging accompaniment to his songs. It is seen mostly in North India.

An officer in the Indian army told me of a similar instrument with only one string that he had come across at Manipur on the Assam frontier, which was played with a bow. It was called *Penna*. The name reminds one of the ancient Pinaka, the stringed instrument of Śiva. Many of these instruments are of the violin variety, and lend support to the idea that the violin in its primitive forms is indigenous to India, and certainly the *Sāraṅgī* and its different varieties show considerable development towards a finer instrument.

The *Rabāb* is a fine Muhammadan instrument, with a wide shallow bowl made of wood covered with parchment. It is something like a flattened and shortened sitār, but has no frets. It has four strings, one of brass and two of gut, with sympathetic metal strings at the side. Sometimes the two upper strings are doubled. All the six strings may be of gut. The instrument is played with a bow of horsehair.

The strings are tuned in one of the following ways:— **Ṡa Pa Ma Sa** (c′ G F C) or **Sa Sa Pa Pa Ma Sa** (c′ c′ G G F C) or **Sa Sa P̱a Ṣa Ga** (C C G_1 C_1 E). Sometimes it has a few catgut frets placed at diatonic intervals. The instrument is found in the Punjab and in Afghanistan, but one rarely sees it to-day. One of the few expert players still in India is in the Rāmpūr State. The great Tān Sen played this instrument. It is a handsome instrument and has a very pleasing tone, somewhat fuller than that of the *Sārangī*. It lends itself to the graces better than the sitār, as it has no frets.

The *Sūr-Śṛingāra* is the modern descendant of the *rabāb*. It was first made by Syed Kalb Ali Khān Bahādur, the late Nawab of Rāmpūr. It is a little longer than the *rabāb*, and the finger-board below the strings is made of metal so that the fingers can easily slide over it. It has a double belly of wood, instead of parchment, as in the *rabāb*, and is played in the same way as the latter. There are eight strings tuned as follows :—**Sa Sa Pa Sa Ga Sa Ri Pa** (C C G_1 C_1 E_1 C D G). The tuning of the seventh and eighth strings varies according to the *rāga*. The first two or three only are used for playing on, and the others are used as the side strings of the vīṇā. It often has a number of sympathetic strings placed underneath, tuned to the intervals of the *rāga* which is being played. Its tone is rich and mellow.

The *Svaramaṇḍala* is the ancient Indian dulcimer. It is said to be the same as the *Kātyāyana-vīṇā*, which was invented by the ṛishi Kātyāyana, and was also called the *Śata-tantrī-vīṇā*, because it had originally hundred strings. Kallinātha, the commentator of *Ratnākara*, says that the *Maṭṭakokila-vīṇā*, mentioned by Śārṅgadeva, is really the *svaramaṇḍala*. The *svaramaṇḍala* is generally made of jackwood and is three feet in length, one and a half feet in breadth and seven inches in height, and it stands on four legs like a piano. Wire strings are used and are attached to round pieces of wood shaped like small chess-pods. The tuning pins are made of wood and are tuned with a key in a similar manner to the pianoforte, that is in semitones.

There are two methods of playing the *svaramaṇḍala*; one, with a mizrab and a shell, the other with two sticks like a xylophone. In the former method, it is played with two plectrums worn upon the first and second fingers of the performer's right hand, while the little finger plays the accompaniment. In the left hand is held a shell which is moved to and fro upon the strings, by which means all Indian musical embellishments can be rendered with great taste and fineness. In the latter method, it is played with two felt-covered sticks and the sound is decidedly like that of a piano.'[1]

This instrument is the forefather of the modern piano, which is nothing more than an enlarged *svaramaṇḍala* in which the strings are struck by mechanical hammers. This instrument, which M. Fredalis calls 'a grand old instrument, whose sweet tones touch the very chords of the heart,' is now forgotten and unused except in a very few places. Its modern representative is the *Qanūn* or *Arramin*, the Indian dulcimer, which is of Persian origin and has only thirty-seven strings, containing three octaves. Some of them are of brass and some of steel. The strings are tuned differently for each *rāga*, so as to reproduce the proper intervals of that *rāga*, and are always played with plectra. Instead of the shell in the left hand, the performer to-day has a small iron ring, with which he produces the various graces. One hearer likened the tone of this instrument to that of an old clavichord.

The *Taush* or *Mayūri* is the peacock fiddle. It is very similar to the sitār and is really a kind of dilruba. It takes its names from the peacock-like resonator.

The Indian Museum, Calcutta, has an interesting collection of primitive stringed instruments containing many others in addition to those given above. None of these primitive instruments are in use to-day, but they are interesting as showing how the present-day stringed instruments developed. The first instrument was the bow with its twanging string, said to be still used on certain occasions by the Nairs of Travancore. Then a number of strings of different lengths were fastened to the same bow. It was then found that by stretching these strings over a hollow body the sound was increased. We find a Burmese instrument with the strings stretched over a hollow body shaped like a boat. One of these specimens has the

[1] From an article by M. Fredalis in *Times of India*, Bombay.

fourteen catgut strings merely tied round the bow, so that it would be most difficult to retune them. A later instrument has developed the tuning peg, fitting into a small hole in the bow. Another type is represented in the *Gabgūki* and *Ānaṇḍa laharī* from the Dekkan. Here the tambourine-like resonator is held under the right arm, and the left hand holds the strings tight, while the fingers of the right hand twang them. The next instrument has a number of thin bamboo rods, which allow the string to be tightened or slackened, and also a tuning peg. This comes from Chota Nagpur and is called *Nandin* or *Gopichand*. A further development in the *Thanthona* from Tanjore shows a round stick fixed in the hollow walls of the cylinder, and carrying two tuning pegs. The *Tsauṅg* from Burma shows another kind of resonator in a hollow piece of bamboo. The strings are narrow strips of bark, carefully sliced off in such a way that the two ends remain attached. They are tightened by pushing a small piece of wood beneath them, and are struck with a plectrum in the right hand. In the middle of the flattened side of the bamboo, there is a rectangular hole covered with a small board of similar shape. This board the player beats with his left thumb, and thus obtains a kind of drum accompaniment. This instrument is still used by the primitive tribes of the Malay Peninsula. Next we see the development of the vīṇā. Here the strings are stretched over a finger-board and kept tight by pegs. This finger-board rests on two or three hollow bodies and the strings are supported on frets. The *Kinnarī* is one of the more primitive instruments of this group [1].

Wind Instruments

It was soon found that stringed instruments were too weak for open air work, and so for this purpose wind instruments came into existence at a very early date. The oldest of all these was probably the buffalo horn,

[1] See *Guide to Musical Instruments exhibited in the Indian Museum*, pp. 4–6.

a specimen of which may be seen in the Indian Museum, and which is still in use in South India. It was not long before the brass horn came into use. Two parts of India, Madras and Nepal, are noted for their brass horns. Practically all those in the Indian Museum came from one or other of these provinces. The name in the north is *Śṛiṅga, Komiki, Kalahāy;* and in the south *Kombu,* which is the Tamil word for 'horn.' These horns are used for signals, processions and festivals. In the south it is often made of several brass pieces, fitting into one another for the sake of portability. It usually has a curved shape, and is about four to six feet in length. It curves in two contrary curves, something like the old curved coach horn. In the south it is only played by the low castes, probably reminiscent of the time when it was always made of horn. It is quite possible to get a large number of notes from it and shrill wavering cadences. I have never heard a melody played upon it. A speciality of Nepal are the snake-shaped horns, with a serpent's or tiger's head as an orifice.

The *Conch Shell* or *Śaṅkhu* is also a very ancient wind instrument and is held very sacred. It is the precursor of the trumpet. One hears of it in all the ancient literature of India, as being used both for warlike and for sacred purposes. To-day it is used a great deal by beggars and in the temples to make a sound which has only occasionally some of the merits of music. It hardly, however, comes under the head of musical instruments. In the temple ritual it either gives an opening fanfare, or plays a sort of rythmical accompaniment.

The *Reed Flute, Vaṅśa* of the ancient books, or *Bāṇsurī,* is one of the commonest instruments in the musical traditions of India. It is also called the *Muralī* or *Fillagorī.* It is always associated with Kṛishṇa, and he is usually represented standing on one leg and playing it. This was the instrument with which Kṛishṇa charmed the gopis of Brindāban. It has various names and forms, and more or less resembles the English flute. It is made from bamboo hollowed out, or else from a hollow piece of metal, and has the usual sound holes. The player blows down the stem and stops the holes as he desires. The *Miy*, another variety, is bored cylindrically and is a regular pastoral instrument.

Mr. Fox Strangways gives a number of flute scales which he found in different parts of India. Many of the intervals were most curious and there was only one which approached the western scale in its intervals. Some of the intervals are quarter tones and some quite strange to our regular tones. One scale ran as follows :—

♭ ♭ ♯
C D♯ F G A B C

The flute is still used to a slight extent both by shepherds and by professional musicians, but it has very largely given way to the reed instruments.

The *Algosa* is a kind of flageolet and has the seven notes of the *gamut*.

The *Kā-sharati* is a flute used in the Khāsi Hills, and the *Basūli* one used in Nepal for weddings and dances.

The *Nāgasara* or *Nāgasuram* is the common reed instrument of India. It is found from north to south, and no wedding procession is complete without it. This instrument is from two to two and a half feet long, and is conical in shape, enlarging downwards. It may be made either of wood or of metal. In the north wood is commonly used, and in the south the best instruments are made of silver. It is pierced with twelve holes, seven of which are used in fingering, the remainder regulating the pitch. Expert players can produce any intervals by only partially covering the available holes. The better instruments, particularly those of silver, have a very fine tone and, heard in the open air, are very attractive. The *nāgasara* performers are often exceedingly expert and are able to produce all the various graces for which Indian music is famous. The melody is clear, interweaved with countless variations. A good *nāgasara* player is in great request and makes a very good living.

The *Niṅkairna* is a kind of small *nāgasara*. It is similar in shape and has the same number of holes. It is a very shrill instrument.

The *Drone* or *Pongi* is an instrument shaped very much like the *nāgasara* and about the same size, except that the conical arrangement is a little larger. Only one note is produced which is called the *Śruti*, that is the key-note or drone to the melody. The instrument has four or five holes, so that the performer can vary the pitch of the note. It is usually played in combination with either the nāgasara or the niṅkairna or with both.

The *Nosbug*, or *Śruti Upāṅga* or *Bhajana Śruti*, is another instrument used almost exclusively for the drone. This is the Indian bagpipe. The bag is made of a kid's skin and is inflated from the mouth. The mouth pieces, of which there are usually two, are of cane, one being smaller than the other. One is used to inflate the bag, and one for playing the drone note. There is usually a little piece of wire or silk tied round the tongue, in order the better to control the sound.

The *Puñji*, or *Jinjīvi* or *Tombi*, is the instrument beloved of jugglers and snake-charmers. The body and mouthpiece are formed from a bottle-shaped gourd, in which are inserted two cane pipes, the interior ends of which are cut so as to form reeds. One of the pipes is pierced with finger holes so that it can be played upon, the other being sounded on the tonic as a drone. The *Puñji* is constructed in the scale of *Bhairavī* (Southern-*Hanumatoḍī*) and is played in the *Nāgavarāḷī rāga*, which is supposed to be peculiarly pleasing to serpents.

An instrument something like this, but having five to nine different reeds inserted into a gourd, is shown in the Indian Museum. The pitch is determined by the length of the reed. This instrument is made on the principle of the organ. It is found among the Assam hill tribes, and it is said that a somewhat similar instrument is found in China.

The *Nallataraṅg* is a pipe instrument, made on the principle of the organ with nineteen pipes. It is played with a bellows, and each pipe is opened by a small key attached to a primitive keyboard.

There are a number of trumpets found in India. The most important of these are the following :—

The *Kuma* is a straight trumpet of brass, and is

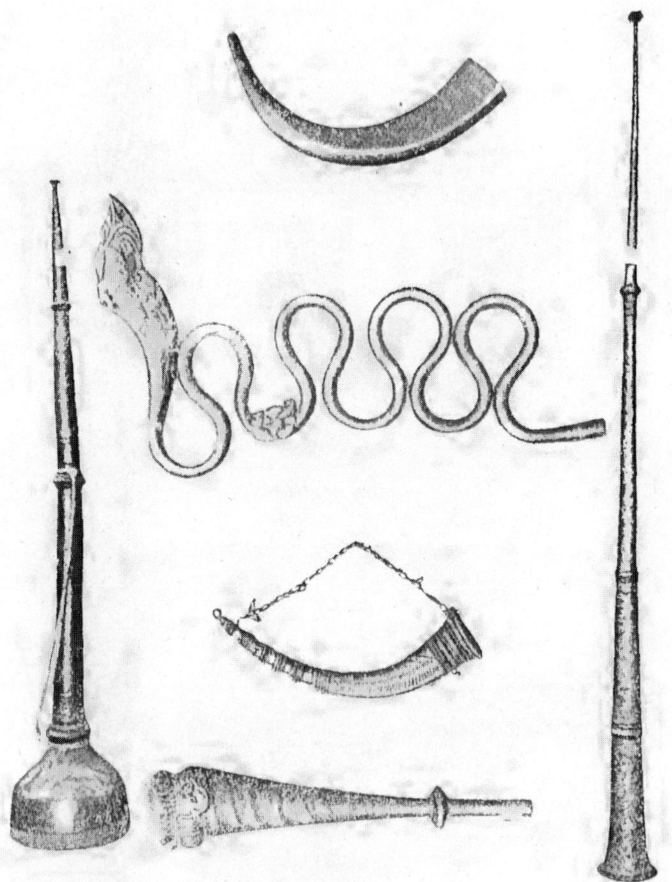

Trumpet. Buffalo horn. Snake-shaped horn. Kombu. Horn with tiger's head. Trumpet.

Some wind instruments

Group of drums

Dholak — Pot-drum, Tomtom — Nagāra, Tabla Pair, Damaru — Dhol, Mṛidaṅga

Bastran (Burmese)

considered very sacred, even Brāhmans being permitted to play it.

The *Tatūri* or *Turahi* is a curved trumpet of brass, like a bugle with one turn. Both this and the *Kuma* are used in religious processions.

The *Sanāi* is a trumpet made from Sisavi wood. It is about one foot long and has seven holes. The player blows straight down the stem.

The *Karaṇa* is a bigger sanāi. The former is used for the two upper registers and the latter for the lower one.

The *Nafari* is a small straight trumpet.

The *Jalataraṅg* and *Kastaraṅg*, though not wind instruments, may come in at this point. The former consists of a number of cups containing varying quantities of water. It is played by dipping the fingers in the water and rubbing them around the rims of the cups. It gives eighteen notes in two octaves. The *Kastaraṅg* is a similar instrument, but no water is placed in the cups which are of different sizes instead. The cups may also be beaten with sticks.

The *Kuṛal* is the panpipe of the shepherds. It consists of a number of hollow reeds or bamboos of different lengths. Its range is extremely limited and the scales use many different kinds of intervals. It is interesting to listen to its shrill tones, with their strange intervals, in the depths of night as the shepherd watches the flocks. I once heard one playing the following notes :—**P d̄ P P P, G M P d̄ P P**

♭ ♭
(G D G G G, E F G D G G.)

INSTRUMENTS OF PERCUSSION

Among these, drums take the first rank. As we have already seen, the drum is one of the most important of India's musical instruments. It provides the tonic to which all the other instruments must be tuned. It is a royal instrument having the right of royal honours. The types of drum used in India are almost innumerable, and it is impossible to give a description of many of them in this book. We can only pick out the most important and describe those. In the Indian Museum, Calcutta, there are altogether 287 different varieties of Indian drums exhibited.

The *Mṛidaṅga* or *Mardala* is the most common and probably the most ancient of Indian drums. It is said to have been invented by Brahma to serve as an accompaniment to the dance of Śiva, in honour of his victory over the three cities; and *Ganeśa*, the son of Śiva, is said to have been the first one to play upon it. The word *mṛidaṅga or mardala* means 'made of clay', and probably therefore its body was originally of mud. Large earthern pots are used even to-day by Indian drummers. They are struck upon the bottom and sometimes a piece of parchment is stretched across the mouth. It is quite a pleasing instrument. There is, however, to-day no clay in the composition of the ordinary *mṛidaṅga*. The *mṛidaṅga* is a barrel-shaped drum about two feet long, with a girth of about three feet in the centre. The two ends have a diameter of about nine inches each. Slight variations from these dimensions may occur in different *mṛidaṅga*. The shape of the *mṛidaṅga* reminds one of two bottomless flower pots joined at the rims. The shell of the drum is now made of wood, and is slightly larger at one end than at the other. The two heads are covered with parchment, which is tightened or loosened by leather braces enclosing small cylindrical blocks of wood, which are either pushed nearer to or further from the head which is being tuned. As the strain on the braces is increased or decreased, so the parchment head is stretched or loosened, and the pitch raised or lowered as desired. On one of these two heads is worked a mixture of manganese dust, boiled rice and tamarind juice, in order to increase the pitch of the note. This appears as a black circle, slightly raised in the centre about one-eighth of an inch. It is a permanent fixture on the drum, and the bare parchment is only left for a very small width around it. The note of this head is Sa and it is played with the fingers of the right hand, which strike it either at the edge or in the centre. The other side of the *mṛidaṅga* is left bare, but on every occasion when it is used, a mixture of boiled rice, water and ashes is put in the centre. This helps to give the dull sound *Pañchama*. It must be carefully washed off every time after it is used. This head is played with the left hand.

The *Tabla* is found in the north and centre of India, where it takes the place of the mṛidaṅga. Instead of being one drum with two heads, it is two drums, the two heads being one on each of the two. They are each slightly smaller in size than the mṛidaṅga, and one of them looks like a mṛidaṅga cut in half. The shape of the *tabla* has been described as 'a great tea-cup and coffee-cup respectively'. One of the drums is sometimes made of copper and the other of wood, or both may be of wood. Both of them have tuning blocks and braces like the mṛidaṅga, or they may have iron screws which work up iron threads. Both heads of the *tabla* have upon them a permanent mixture. On the left hand drum it is worked on slightly to one side and for about two inches in diameter. On the other head it is the same as upon the right head of the mṛidaṅga. The smaller *tabla* is sometimes called *Bāhya*, though this is really a small wooden kettle drum of similar shape. Both the mṛidaṅga and *tabla* are essentially concert drums and lend themselves to all kinds of drumming finesse. The mṛidaṅga is used mostly in the south of India, though it is also found in the north. The *tabla* is rarely found further south than Bangalore.

The *Pakhawāj* is a drum slightly larger than the mṛidaṅga but similar in shape, which is used in the north of India.

The *Nagāra*, or *Bherī* or *Nakkāra*, is a large kettle drum, used very largely for war-like and religious ceremonies. It is called *Dundubhi* in the ancient literature. The shell is made of copper, brass or sheet-iron rivetted together. The heads are made of skin and are stretched upon hoops of metal. The head may be anything from two to three feet in diameter. It is beaten with two curved sticks.

The *Mahānagāra* or *Nahabet* is a very large drum of this sort used in wandering theatrical troupes, or by the great Muhammadan nobles in their ceremonies. It is sometimes five feet in diameter.

The *Karadsamila* is another form of this drum used in Lingāyat temples. It is slightly larger and the shell is conical, with the apex flattened. The head of this drum is braced by leather thongs round the shell. The skin is often put on when wet and then shrunk into its place.

The *Dhol* is the wedding drum of India. It is cylindrical in shape and about twenty inches long and twelve inches in diameter. It is made of wood bored out of the solid. The heads are made of skin and are stretched by hoops fastened to the shell and strained by interlaced thongs of leather bound round the shell. A band of leather passes round the shell in the middle and serves to tighten up the instrument to the desired pitch. A mixture of boiled rice and wood ash is often applied to the ends of the *dhol* to give more resonance. This drum is played either by hand or with sticks. Sometimes both are used. If by hand, it is struck by the palm. The sound is a hollow bang with very little music in it, and there is no possibility of drumming finesse, as there is with the mṛidaṅga. The *dhol* is often used in temples at ceremonies and festivals.

The *Dholki*, *Dholak* and *Dāk* are smaller and larger kinds of *dhol* respectively. The former is used by the Dekkan women.

The *Damaru*, *Nidukku*, *Udukku* or *Budbudaka* is a peculiar drum, shaped like an hour-glass. A small stick or a piece of lead or a pea is attached to a string, which is wound round the middle. It is held in the right hand, so that the squeeze of the fingers tightens the braces and sharpens the tone a little within a sixth. The stick or piece of lead or pea strikes on the drum heads alternately, as the holder turns the drum this way and that. This drum is said to have been used by Śiva. To-day, however, it is the possession of beggars and snakecharmers and their ilk.

The *Edaka* or *Dudi* is a metal drum of this same shape and size used in Coorg. One end of it is beaten by a drumstick and one by hand. In Malabar a drum of this sort is made from a gourd. When four or five of them are beaten together at a religious service the noise is prodigious. They have practically no musical value.

The *Karadivādya* is a large-sized variety of the same kind of drum, which is beaten with a padded drum stick.

The *Udupe* is a goblet shaped drum used by the Lingāyats of Mysore in their religious ceremonies.

In addition to these, there are the various *Tomtoms*, both large and small, used throughout India, particularly for proclamations of Government orders and sales and so on. They are beaten with small wooden sticks.

Various kinds of tambourines are used. There is the circular *Thambatti* of South India, the large *Dāmphu* of Nepal, and the little *Khañjeri* of Madras, the latter very much like the western tambourine. There are also some known by the very appropriate name of *Ḍiṇḍimi*.

Various kinds of cymbals are also in use. There are the simple kind made of brass, copper or bronze, called *Kaitāla* or *Jālrā* or *Mañjīva*. One of them is held tightly in the left hand and the other loosely in the right. The time is expressed with many modulations of tone and varieties of beat. They are by no means easy to play, and experts produce with them most intricate and delicate movements, all in perfect harmony with the time of the music.

There are also large cymbals called *Jharīgha* which are used especially in temples.

There is a peculiar kind of metal cymbal used in Bundelkand. It is called *Chintlā* and consists of two flat pieces of iron two feet long with pointed ends, held together at the other end by a ring of iron having a few smaller rings attached to it. The two pointed ends are beaten together and the rings are also struck on to the iron in time with the beats.

Various kinds of castinets are used throughout India.

The *Kustar* or *Chittika* consist of two pieces of hard wood about six inches in length, flat on one side and rounded on the other. Clusters of bells on small pieces of metal are placed at the ends, and these make a musical jingle when the *Kustar* is shaken. A ring is usually inserted at the back of each for the finger to pass through. They are held in the one hand, and the flat surfaces are beaten together by alternately closing and opening the fingers.

The *Kartāl* are large *Kustar* with two pairs of cymbals and holes in the wood for the fingers to pass through so as to grip the instrument.

Chakra are circular wooden castinets made with slightly concave surfaces. They are also called *Khattalā*. Another strange form of percussion instrument which still lingers in Burma is the *Bastran*. It is a kind of boatshaped melodion, with twenty-five bamboos of different lengths for the note keys.

CHAPTER VIII

INDIAN AND WESTERN MUSIC

CAPTAIN DAY, whose example might well be followed by other military men in India, says:—

> Almost every traveller in India comes away with the idea that the music of the country consists of mere noise and nasal drawling of the most repulsive kind, often accompanied by contortions and gestures of the most ludicrous description. But in certainly two-thirds of such cases, the singing and dancing witnessed has been of the commonest, and the performers of the most abandoned and depraved of the city; and the traveller has therefore received a false impression, which may abide through life, or impede the progress of a more correct appreciation of the real value of Indian music. But it is hardly fair that an art so little really understood, even among the natives of India themselves, should be judged by such a criterion and then put aside as worthless, because solitary individuals have been deceived by parties of outcast charlatans whose object is mere gain. For that Indian music is an art, and a very intricate and difficult one too, can hardly be denied. But to appreciate it one must first put away all thought of European music and then judge of it by an Indian standard, and impartially upon its own merits; of the ingenuity of the performer, the peculiar rhythm of the music, the extraordinary scales used, the recitatives, the amount of imitation, the wonderful execution and memory of the performer, and his skill in employing small intervals as grace. Then when we hear old slokas and ghazals, songs written hundreds of years ago, sung with the same sweet dreamy cadences, the same wild melody, to the same soft beats of little hands, and the same soft timkle of the silver cymbals, we shall perhaps begin to feel that music of this kind can be as welcome and tasteful to ears accustomed to it as the music of the West, with its exaggerated sonorousness, is to us; and so our contempt will gradually give way to wonder, and upon acquaintance possibly to love. For this music, let us remember daily gives pleasure to as many thousands as its more cultivated European sister gives to hundreds. There is hardly any festivity in India in which some part is not assigned to music, and for religious ceremonies its use is universal.'

In judging of Indian music one must enquire whether it contains those musical qualities which ensure an artistic appreciation from the cultured. When discussing this matter with an acquaintance once he said to me, 'There ought to be something in all good music which any cultured ear and mind can artistically appreciate.' He was of course referring to the best examples of either western or eastern music and to cultured minds on both sides of the world. The question naturally arises here as to whether it is possible for any one to appreciate the music of the other side without some special education of the musical faculty. We know how difficult it is for people who have had no musical education at all to appreciate classical music in the west, and we know too that all classes can be educated to appreciate it. It is a fact that many musical artists of the west have revealed a very keen appreciation of Indian music, and some of them have learnt to use it with real distinction. Some may think that this is a rare occurrence, and not a possibility for every-one who has a soul for music. This book should at any rate reveal the fact that Indian music, whether fully developed or not, is at least founded on sound musical principles, and that it does contain possibilities of appreciation by all truly musical people.

There are many reasons which prevent people from giving that appreciation to the music of the other people which it merits. There are some to whom the music of the other is simply a noise more or less disagreeable, or perhaps 'the least disagreeable of noises.' There are some who like Aurangzeb would have Indian music buried so deep that 'neither voice nor echo shall issue from the grave.' Various causes may conduce to this lack of appreciation. A writer in the *Madras Mail* sometime ago gave expression to one of these. He wrote:

> 'I own that Indian music, though it interests me, does not appeal to me in the least. I have tried again and again to catch some comprehensive idea and grasp a beginning or an ending, to discover whether the music is pathetic or sublime, erotic or religious, and I have never yet succeeded.'

He goes on to say with impartial fairness:

> 'The conclusion to be drawn is not that the art is inferior or that it does not exist. It is the ears of our musical understanding which are deaf to those sounds, which have so powerful an effect upon our neighbours.'

There are also those who are repelled by the grotesque exhibitions, which so often accompany the rendering of Indian music even by some of the best artists, though this is not a trait which is altogether confined to Indian artists. I remember a story which will illustrate this point very well, and which incidentally shows that cultured Indians as well find them grotesque. A foolish shepherd became suddenly rich, and one day a musician came and sang before him, shaking his head, eyes and hands in time with the music as he did so, and making the most grotesque faces. The shepherd not having seen that kind of thing before thought that he had fits and took him inside and had him branded. The musician was glad to get away. Still he went on with his art, and one day, when singing before a king, the king was so pleased that he went away to get him a valuable present. The musician thinking of his former experience, ran off. Then the king sent to his house and asked what was the matter, and was informed of the treatment he had formerly received. The king replied, 'A fool may acquire riches, but does not therefore become sensible.' Another story on the same theme tells of a musician singing before a shepherd, with similar strange gestures. The shepherd wept copiously all the time. The musician, being unable to understand the cause of his weeping, stopped and asked him why he was weeping. The shepherd said, 'Last night one of my sheep had the same disease and swelled up and died. When I think that you too will die in four watches, it makes me sad to think of one so young suffering from such a dire disease.' This story shows that it is not only the European who can look upon these things with a sense of humour. To allow this kind of thing to prevent our appreciation of the music is to lose the substance because of its covering. One may hope that it will not be long before in India itself these grotesque contortions will be condemned as bad form by the best people.

Then, as Captain Day says, there are many who condemn Indian music without having made any genuine attempt to understand or appreciate it. They take all their ideas of it from the indifferent barber's band, or the wandering troupe with its noisy instruments. They are encased in their prejudice, which forms a tough skin and prevents them from feeling any sense of the beauty and charm of the music. One can only hope that some day they will wake up to the fact that prejudice is farthest removed from discrimination, and that it has resulted not only in their loss but also in a loss to all, inasmuch as it has hampered a real appreciation of things Eastern. Strange though it may appear, there are many Indians who feel just the same about western music. An Indian gentleman in Lahore remarked to me that western music to him was like 'the howling of a jackal in a desert.' One is glad to know that there are to-day an increasing number of both westerners and easterners who are learning to appreciate the charm and the art of the music of the other.

It would be well now to gather together some of the important distinctions between Indian and western music.

1. The dominant factor in Indian music is melody, while that of western music is harmony. In the one case notes are related to definite notes of a *rāga*, and in the other case to varying chords. Indian melody is produced by the regulated succession of concordant notes, while western harmony arises from the agreeable concord of various related notes. As a result of this differentiation, Indian music has developed solely along the lines of melody, while the greatest development of western music has taken place in the region of harmony. Does the fact that western music has developed a second dimension, so to speak, make it more advanced than Indian music? Can we call Indian music thereby inferior or primitive? Indian music has taken one line of development, that of melody; and, in order to add to its charm and variety, has developed every phase of it, including time-measure, in ways that have never occurred to the western mind. These are two lines of development, and perhaps one has travelled as far along its line, as the other upon its line. There has been far more development in Indian music, than even many Indian musicians were aware of; as until recently there was no opportunity for the different lines of development to converge or to co-operate with each other, owing to the enormous distances, the

absence of the habit of wide travel, and the lack of facilities for intercommunication. However, things are rapidly changing, and to-day we have a permanent all-India organisation, which will undoubtedly gather together the scattered lines of development and bring them to bear upon Indian music as a whole. It is only recently that musical associations have been formed in India, and that music lovers have had opportunity to get together and compare their work. All this must be remembered in judging the progress that has been made by Indian music. Another thing that has greatly hampered this progress has been the absence of an adequate and universal system of notation. This too is being remedied, and it will be possible soon to judge the relative progress of western and Indian systems of music on a basis of equality.

2. Then again, Indian melody is cast in one definite mood throughout, and both time and tune are wrought into one homogeneous whole. Variations are not allowed to alter that mood, which persists with the *rāga*. The balance of the music is obtained partly by time-variations and partly by grace. 'In western music mood is used to articulate the balance of the whole piece.' The particular times for singing the different *rāgas*, the *rāga* pictures and the emotions associated with them all fit into this idea of the Indian melody.

3. Then again, and perhaps most important of all, in Indian music the salient notes are fixed by long association and tradition, and any alteration of such saliency is not as a rule possible in a melody. The relation of the individual notes to one another is settled by ancient tradition. In western music, on the other hand, the salient notes are made by the momentary impulse of the harmony or of the counterpoint, and it is the cluster of notes rather than the individual note which has special value.

'In Indian music the notes are members of a form already supplied by tradition, and the newness is created by their arrangement and graces, while in western music they create new forms as the music proceeds.

'In Indian music the notes stand out from each other as clearly as do the faces of our friends in our mind.'

4. Further in Indian composition the melody is dependent upon the relation to certain fixed notes which vary according to the *rāga*. It sets no store by any progress through notes which suggest harmony, whereas western melodies tend to circle round the notes which are harmonically related to the tonic. As a result imitation at different levels, so common in western music, is very rarely found in Indian music, and the two tetrachords are seldom identical in the character of their constituents.

5. As we have seen Indian music lays great stress on grace-gamaka—'curves of sound.' These are not mere accidental ornaments as in western music, but essential parts of the melodic structure.

6. The use of microtones in Indian music and the general absence of the tempered scale gives a very distinct flavour to it. To those whose ears have always been tuned to certain fixed intervals, this occurrence of quite different intervals, some of them most strange to western ears, alters the whole feeling of the music. Mrs. Mann says, 'Western music is music without microtones, as Indian music is music without harmony.'

7. We have already noticed the difference in time-measures and this is accountable to a very considerable extent for the strangeness of Indian music to so many. Varieties of duration do not come naturally to ears which are habituated to varieties of accent.[1]

8. Another difference that has a great deal to do with our appreciation or otherwise of music, is the matter of emphasis upon certain external qualities. Western music rightly has come to lay very great emphasis upon tone and timbre, whereas Indian music passes these by on the other side and gives all attention to execution and accuracy. The melody is not determined by canons of charm or pleasure, but by adherence to certain fixed standards; and the quality of tone in which the melody is sung or played does not have the importance that it does in the west. 'The Indian singer is first a musician and secondly

[1] See page 73.

a voice-producer. He is not singing from some set piece, but extemporizing according to some definite rule, which almost unconsciously models the form of his song.' This accounts for the frequent occurrence even in the best songs of difficult sol-fa passages which have no musical beauty whatever. A short time ago while talking with an Indian musical friend about a certain singer, I said, 'He has not got a very good voice.' 'Oh,' said my friend, 'That is nothing. The great thing is for him to sing correctly and skilfully. The tone does not matter at all.' In a note in the *Adyar Bulletin*, Madras, somewhat recently, Mr. Tagore, in discussing the singing of an Indian lady, who had received training in Europe, said that in India any finesse in singing is regarded with contempt, no trouble being taken to make either voice or manner attractive. He goes on:

'They are not ashamed if their gestures are violent, their top notes cracked, and their bass notes unnatural. They take it to be their sole function to display their perfect mastery over all the intricacies of times and tunes, forms and formalities of the classic traditions.'

A commentator adds, 'In Europe we listen for the tone, the sweetness of the voice, of the instrument. In India they listen only for the tune—the melody and the rhythm.' It must, however, be added that to-day many Indian music-lovers are coming to realize the importance of tone, and are placing very much greater emphasis upon it.

One thing which often depresses the western listener is the harsh nasal tone of the Indian singer. It is interesting to find that, while many Indians are trying to get away from it, the nasal tone still has its defenders. Mrs. Mann says that it is a degraded form of a very fine tradition, to the effect that the yogi could obtain the power to go on singing without breathing, and it is the desire to attain to this power which is responsible for the cultivation of the habit of singing at the back of the nose.

Sir Rabindranath Tagore goes down to the fundamental causes of the difference between the music of East and West

'At first, I must admit your Western music jarred upon me. I heard Madame Albani sing a song in which there was an imitation of the nightingale. It was so childishly imitative of the mere externals of nature that I could take little pleasure in it.'

'And what food for musical inspiration would a Hindu find in the song of the nightingale?' asked the questioner. 'He would find the soul-state of the listener; he would make music in the same way that Keats wrote his ode. It seems to me that Indian music concerns itself more with human experience as interpreted by religion, than with experience in an everyday sense. For us, music has above all a transcendental significance. It disengages the spiritual from the happenings of life; it sings of the relationship of the human soul with the soul of things beyond. The world by day is like European music; a flowing concourse of vast harmony, composed of concord and discord and many disconnected fragments. And the night world is our Indian music; one pure, deep and tender *rāga*. They both stir us, yet the two are contradictory in spirit. But that cannot be helped. At the very root nature is divided into two, day and night, unity and variety, finite and infinite. We men of India live in the realm of night; we are overpowered by the sense of the One and Infinite. Our music draws the listener away beyond the limits of everyday human joys and sorrows, and takes us to that lonely region of renunciation which lies at the root of the universe, while European music leads us a variegated dance through the endless rise and fall of human grief and joy.'

On the same subject Mr. Fox Strangways says:

'One shows a rejection of what is transient, a soberness in gaiety, endurance in sorrow, a search after the spiritual ideals of life. The other shows a vivid insight, an eager quest after wayside beauty and the dexterous touch that turns it to account. The one seems to say, 'Life is puzzling, its claims are many, but we will hammer out a solution, not by turning away from ugliness, but by compelling it to serve the ends of beauty.' The other, 'Life is simple and beauty close at hand at every moment, wherever we go; the mistake is in ourselves if we do not train our eyes and ears and hearts to find it.' (F.S. pp. 339, 340).

Mrs. Mann says in the same strain:

'While western music speaks of the wonders of God's creation, eastern music hints at the inner beauty of the Divine in man and in the world. Indian music requires of its hearers something of that mood of divine discontent, of yearning for the infinite and impossible.'

Another writer remarks:

An Indian banquet with its vast variety of dishes of every taste and savour, is bewildering to the European who enjoys eating one thing at a time, with his whole gastric soul concentrated on it. Similarly the European's multiplicity of sounds in music bewilders the Indian, who likes to elaborate one particular melody to what seems to the western tedious lengths.' (I.S.R., Sept. 21,1920.)

One can only say further that it is not impossible for every one who has an ear and heart for musical beauty to learn to appreciate the charm of Indian music and in some measure to understand it ; and that this attitude is far more productive of joy to oneself and to others, than the more common attitude of insular prejudice which refuses to think that there is any possibility of finding something worth appreciating in the music of India. While a good deal of training would probably be required before one could appreciate all the niceties of the classical style, it should not be difficult for any westerner to appreciate heartily the beautiful songs and melodies of good Indian musicians. We would also urge that Indian musicians should make a point of studying the principles and history of western music. The experience of the west will be of immense help to musical progress in India.

The deeper spirit of nationalism and religion shows itself in music as much, if not more than in other things. Music has a sacred purpose connected with the regeneration of the human heart, and plays an important part in almost all our dealings in the world. If, however, Indian music is to advance and to become the vehicle for the expression of the highest ideals and feelings of modern India, it needs men like Bach and Beethoven, to lead it forward and to organize it, and to give of their best to its study and application. When people are too occupied with the sciences and arts which lead to worldly prosperity, devotion to the cultural arts finds no place. Mahārāja Tagore, at a lecture in Calcutta, asked those who would do something for Indian music to give more attention to the grammar of music, to the proper theory of *rāga* and *tāla*, and not simply to churn out of their minds anything which appeared to them to be music, in accordance with notions derived from street singers or from tradition. The science and practice of Indian music, if it is to advance, needs a great deal of original research, as well as very thorough education. Such research and cultivation of Indian music means the giving up of time and energy now spent on money-making to musical culture. It needs also the daring which, while based on a thorough knowledge of the science as it exists to-day, refuses to be handicapped by traditions which belong to yesterday.

There are various practical ways in which enthusiasts can help in the progress and development of Indian music. The first thing to do is to study and practice it for oneself. There are books to-day, both in English and the vernaculars, which will help in this. Then it is good to make a habit of training the children in Indian music, and to see that they can play at least one Indian instrument. Every cultured family in the west aims at this, and in the large towns of India at any rate it is becoming quite possible to-day.

It is possible also to render aid to the different musical societies which are growing up. Princes and wealthy men can liberally help the All-India Music Conference and the Academy of Indian Music now established in Delhi with its ambitious programme.

We can also help in a great extension of musical knowledge among the people generally. There was in the last half of the nineteenth century a great growth of musical knowledge in England, largely through voluntary associations, which grew up all over the country. The different musical festivals which were organized also contributed much to this; and there seems no reason why, in association with some of the annual festivals of India, there should not be organized musical festivals, which would attract artists and choirs from all over the country.

The ancient Greeks are said to have made a point of teaching their children music, because they believed that it made them more unselfish, and helped them to see better the beauty of order and the usefulness of rule. Lord Lamington, Governor of Bombay, at the opening of the Gāndharva Mahāvidyālaya, said:

> 'Music has in the past played a part in the education of the people of India. I believe that it may do much more in the future if it is made an object of reverential study, and thrown open to far greater numbers than at present, and if it is allowed to take its proper place as an elevating influence.'

In music, as in all other things in India, co-operation and real comradeship between East and West is needed, if the greatest possible progress is to be made. The words of Lord Ronaldshay, Governor of Bengal, apply to culture as well as to government in India. 'The future of the land we live in may be likened to a splendid edifice built up on a firm foundation of pillared arches. The pillars are the two great races, whose lot has been so strangely intertwined by the fingers of Providence—the Indians and the British. The keystones of the arches are the will on the part of both races to understand and co-operate with one another in this task.'

The morning will surely come, the darkness will vanish, and thy voice pour down in golden streams breaking through the sky.

Then thy words will take wing in songs from every one of my birds' nests, and thy melodies will break forth in flowers in all my forest groves

RABINDRANATH TAGORE.

APPENDIX I

BIBLIOGRAPHY OF INDIAN MUSIC

(Works in English only)

1. *Universal History of Music*, by Rajah S. M. Tagore, Mus. Doc., Calcutta.

An interesting compendium of musical knowledge with a valuable chapter on the *Music of India*. (*Out of print.*)

2. *Hindu Music*, compiled by Rajah S. M. Tagore. By various authors. Calcutta, 1875. Bābu Punchanan Mukerji, pp. viii. 308.

A collection of essays by well-known Oriental scholars on different aspects of Indian music. (*Out of print.*)

3. *The Six Principal Rāgas*, by Rajah S. M. Tagore, Calcutta, 1877. Calcutta Central Press Co., Ltd., pp. 46 xii.

Gives a general introduction to Indian musical theory, with detailed descriptions of the six rāgas. With six fine plates representing the rāga pictures. (*Out of print.*)

4. *The Music and Musical Instruments of Southern India and the Deccan*, by Captain C. R. Day, London, 1891, pp. xvi. 173. 17 coloured plates.

A good general introduction to southern music, with detailed descriptions of musical instruments and some fine coloured plates. Very valuable book. (*Out of print.*)

5. *Oriental Music in Staff Notation*, by A. H. Chinnaswamy Mudaliar, Madras, 1892, pp. 36, 106. Obtainable for Rs. 9 a copy from Miss Miriam Raju, San Thomé, Madras.

It deals entirely with Carnatic music. The introduction is elementary, giving information concerning the principles of South Indian music. The longer part of the book is taken up with examples from the great masters of the south written in staff notation, and also a few folk songs.

6. *Indian Music*, by Bhavānrāo A. Pingle, of Kathiawād, Byculla, 1898, pp. xviii. 341. Second edition.

A good account of the music of North India with a few examples. A mine of information on many details of performance.'

(*Out of print.*)

7. *A Short Account of the Hindu System of Music*, by A. C. Wilson (Lady), Lahore, 1904, pp. 48. Gulab Singh & Sons, Lahore.

An elementary account of Hindusthani music. Has a good glossary.

8. *Indian Music*, by Ananda Coomaraswamy, 1917, G. Schirmer, New York and London. Reprinted from the *Musical Quarterly*, April 1917, pp. 9.

9. *Indian Music*, by Shahinda (Begum Fyzee-Rahamin) with preface by F. Gilbert Webb, 1914. William Marchant & Co., London, pp. 96.

A general account of Hindusthani music, with descriptions of a number of Hindusthani rāgas and with a number of rāga pictures.

10. *Notes on the Principles of Hindu Music*, by E. Stradiot. With a collection of nine Hindu melodies. From the Madras Journal of Literature and Science for 1887–88, pp. 28.

A very slight account of southern music.

11. *Indian Music*, by A. K. Coomaraswamy, an essay in the *Dance of Siva*, by the same author, pp. 72–81, 5 plates.

An interesting description.

12. *Art Manufacture in India*, by T. N. Mukharji, F.L.S., Indian Museum, Calcutta. Specially compiled for Glasgow International Exhibition, 1888, Calcutta, 1888. Superintendent of Government Printing, pp. 451. *Musical Instruments of India*, pp. 76–96.

13. *First Steps in Hindu Music*, by H. P. Krishna Rao, Mysore, 1906. Weekes & Co., London, pp. 52.

A very elementary work with a small collection of South Indian melodies in staff notation.

14. *Essays on National Idealism*, by A. K. Coomaraswamy, Colombo, 1909.

About twenty pages on *Indian Music*.

15. *Some Thoughts on Hindi Music*, by G. S. Khare, Poona, 1912. Arya Bhushan Press, Poona, pp. 16.

A paper read before the Literary and Philosophical Club, Poona. A slight discussion on the śrutis.

16. *The Hindu Musical Scale*, by K. B. Deval, Poona, 1910. Arya Bhushan Press, Poona, pp. viii. 49. With an introduction by Mr. E. Clements.

Deals only with the theory of the twenty-two śrutis.

17. *Theory and Practice of Hindu Music*, by C. Gangadhar, Madras, pp. 40. Methodist Publishing House, Madras. Obtainable at C. Ramachandar, 25 Perumal Koil Garden Street, Georgetown, Madras.

A very elementary and superficial account of Carnatic music. Specially meant for instruction in playing the vīṇā.

18. *Introduction to the Study of Indian Music*, by E. Clements, London, 1913. Longmans, Green & Co., pp. xv. 104.

A technical discussion of the Grāmas and Śrutis. With a glossary. Contains translations from *Nāṭya Śāstra* and *Sangīt-Ratnākara*.

19. *Some Indian Conceptions of Music*, by Mrs. Maud Mann. 1911–12, pp. 41. Proceedings of the Musical Association.

Gives an account of the Carnatic system.

20. *The Indian Music Journal*, Editor, H. P. Krishna Rao, Mysore. Bi-monthly. Two volumes only, 1912–13. Crown Press, Mysore.

Contains much valuable and interesting information and a translation of portions of the *Rāgavibodha*.

21. *Contribution to the Study of Ancient Hindu Music*, by Rao Sahib P. R. Bhandarkar, Indore, 1912. British Indian Press, Mazgaon, Bombay. Reprinted from

the *Indian Antiquary*, Vol. xli. July, August and November 1912.

A discussion on the śrutis. Also contains the Kudumiyamāmalai inscription on Indian music, probably of the seventh century.

22. *The Music of Hindostan*, by A. H. Fox Strangways. Clarendon Press, Oxford, 1914, pp. 364.

Deals primarily with Hindusthani music, but also contains much valuable information on Carnatic music. The only thoroughly scientific treatise on the subject by an expert in western music and a keen student of Indian music, who had splendid opportunities of hearing and studying the best Indian music. Contains a good glossary and index.

23. *The Hindu Scale*, by A. H. Fox Strangways in Sammelbande dere Internationalen in Musik-Gesellschaft, 1907-08, pp. 449–516, Bräitkopf & Hartel, Leipzig.

Treats of the underlying principles of Indian melodies and the connection between Greek and Indian music.

24. *The Psychology of Music*, by H. P. Krishna Rao, Mysore, 1916. Wesleyan Mission Press, Mysore, pp. 71, Re. 1-4-0.

An interesting description of the emotions associated with musical notes and melodies.

25. *Theory of Indian Music as expounded by Somanātha*, by K. B. Deval, Poona, 1916. Arya Bhushan Press, Poona. pp. 64.

An introduction to the musical scale of India and an explanation, according to the author's view, of many verses from the *Rāgavibodha*. His explanation is not accepted by other scholars and musicians.

26. *Report of First Indian Musical Conference*. Held at Baroda in 1916. Published at Baroda, 1917. Baroda Printing Works. pp. 63

Contains summaries of papers and discussions.

27. *Indian Music*, by Mrs. R. M. Dunkelberger, Rentichintala. Article in Gospel Witness, Guntur. February 1917.

A general account of Indian music.

28. *Guide to the Musical Instruments in the Indian Museum, Calcutta*, by Dr. A. M. Meerwarth, 1917. Government Printing, Calcutta. pp. 33. As. 8.

An account of the very fine collection of Indian musical instruments in the Indian Museum, Calcutta, with pictures of many of them.

29. *Hindu Music* by C. Tirumalayya Naidu, M. R. A. S., Madras, 1896. pp. 37. Vijayanti Press, Madras.

An English introduction under this title in a book by the above author entitled, *Gāna Vidya Sanjīvinī*.

30. *A Short Historical Survey of the Music of Upper India*, by N. V. Bhatkhande, B.A., B.L., Bombay, 1917. Published by Karkhoro Maneckji Minocher-Honjj of Bombay, Samachar. pp. 52. Reprint of a paper read at the All-India Music Conference at Baroda, 1916.

A very interesting account of the development of Hindusthani Music, containing results of original research, and a discussion on the best line of advance in Indian musical theory. A very valuable work by a scholar and a practical musician, with suggestions for a new classification of Hindusthani rāgas.

31. *Karunānamṛita Sāgaram*, by Rao Sahib Abraham Paṇḍither, Tanjore, 1918. pp. Lawley Electric Printing Press, Tanjore.

A technical and abstruse account of the development of South Indian Rāgas, with special reference to the author's peculiar theory and to ancient Tamil works.

32. *Indian Music.*, Young Men of India, May 1918, Calcutta.

Contains a number of articles on Indian Music, including one by Mr. Fox Strangways, and one by Professor Percy Brown on '*Visualised Music.*'

33. *Travancore Music and Musicians*, by T. Lakshmana Pillay, Trivandrum, 1918. Included in collection of essays published by the author. pp. 93–133.

A historical essay of some interest.

34. *Report of the Second All-India Music Conference.* Held at Delhi, December 1918. By the Honorary Secretary 1919. pp. 60 with four appendices and many photos.

A very valuable account of the proceedings and good summaries of the papers.

APPENDIX II

GLOSSARY OF INDIAN MUSICAL TERMS

The numbers are those of the pages

The term southern or northern placed after a meaning indicates that the word is used in that sense only in the south or north respectively.

Abhaṅga ...	... Marāṭhī devotional song, 92.
Ābhog ...	... Closing section of a Hindusthani song, 87.
Adhvadarśak	... Name given to Ma, 63.
Āditāla ...	... Three-beat time, southern, 75, 76.
Akshara ...	... Syllable unit of time-measure, 73.
Ākshiptikā	... Third section of Ālāphana, 86.
Alaṅkāra ...	... Graces and ornaments of melody.
Ālāphana, Ālāp	... Improvised introduction to a melody, 86.
Algosa ...	... A flute, 117.
Amṛita ...	... A musical instrument, 100.
Aṁśa ...	... Prominent note of a rāga. Also called Vādī, 39.
Ānanda laharī	... An ancient bow instrument, 115.
Āndolitam	... A gamaka, the swing, 85.
Aṅga ...	... The tetrachord. A member of a time beat, 6, 74.
Antarā ...	... Second section of northern melody, 87.
Antara ...	... Sharp of Ga, southern, 13.
Anudātta...	... A member of the Sāman chant, a falling tone, 27.
Anudruta ...	... Smallest time measure. One akshara, 73.
Anumandaram	... Fourth string of vīṇā, 104.
Anupallavi	... Second section of a Carnatic melody, 87.
Anuvādī ...	... Imperfect consonance, 26.
Apsaras ...	... Heavenly dancers, 7.
Arramin ...	... Svaramaṇḍala, dulcimer, 114.
Ārya ...	... An ancient Sanskrit metre.
Ārohaṇa ...	... Complete ascent of the gamut, 85.
Ās ...	... A slide, northern, 84.
Astāī ...	... First section of Hindusthani melody, 87.
Aṭa tāla ...	... Four-beat time, southern, 75.
Aṭa-chautāla	... Crooked four-beat time, northern, 76.
Atikomal ...	... Double flat, 4.
Atikrama ...	... Disjunct motion, thirds, fourths and fifths in Sāman chant.
Atisvārya ...	... Sixth note of Sāman scale, 27, 30.
Atitīvra ...	... Double sharp, 4.
Avarohaṇa	... Complete descent of gamut, 85.
Āvarta ...	... Complete section of time-measure, 6, 74.

Bāhya ... ... Small drum, 121.
Bālasarasvatī ... Southern form of tambūr, 111.
Bāṇsurī ... ... A flute, 116.
Bastran ... ... Burmese melodion, 124.
Basūli ... ... Nepālī flute, 117.
Baul ... ... Bengālī folk music, 92.
Bhajana ... ... A form of musical entertainment. A band, 91.
Bhajana śruti ... Drone instrument, 118.
Bherī ... ... Nagāra drum, 121.
Bilampet ... ... Slow speed, adagio, northern, 78
Bīṇ ... ... Northern name of vīṇā, 102.
Bol ... ... Drum-stroke syllables, 81.
Boljhārā ... ... A musical passage in arpeggio, 85.
Brahmā-vīṇā ... Variety of tambūr, 111.
Budbudaka ... Small drum like hour-glass, 122.

Chakra ... ... Circular wooden castanets, 122.
Chāpu ... ... A syncopated time-measure, 77.
Charaṇam ... Third section of southern melody, 87.
Chārtāla ... ... Four-beat time, northern, 81.
Chatuḥśruti ... Name given to first sharp note of Ri and Dha in south, 3.
Chaturaṅga ... A form of melodic composition, 90.
Chaturtha... ... Fourth note of Sāman scale, 27, 30.
Chatusra ... ... A Jātī in time-measure, 75.
Chautāla ... ... Same as Chārtāla, 81, 88.
Chikāra ... ... A musical instrument like Sāraṅgī, 100, 109.
Chikāri ... ... Side strings of vīṇā and similar instruments, 104.
Chintlā ... ... Curious iron cymbals of Central India, 123.
Chittika ... ... Castanets, 123.
Chyuta ... ... Ancient name for certain śrutis, literally 'fallen.'

Dādrā ... ... A Hindusthani melody, 90. A syncopated time, northern, 76.
Dāk ... ... A large dhol, a drum, 122.
Dāmphu ... ... Tambourine, 123.
Damaru ... ... A small drum, 122.
Dhamār ... ... A four-beat time, northern, 76, 89.
Dhaivata ... ... Sixth note of the octave, 3, 33.
Dheṅka ... ... Form of Kinnarī, 112.
Dhīma ... ... A four-beat time, northern, 76, 88.
Dhol ... ... A drum, 122.
Dholak ... ... A drum, 122.
Dholki ... ... A small dhol, 122.
Dhrupad ... ... A northern form of song, 87.
Dhruva ... ... Four-beat time, southern, 75.
Dhun ... ... A northern popular song, 89.
Dilruba ... ... A stringed instrument, 107.
Ḍiṇḍimi ... ... Tambourine, 123.

Dīpachandī ... A four-beat time-measure, northern, 89.
Dṛitakāla ... Quick speed, allegro, 78.
Drone ... A reed instrument, 118.
Druta ... A time beat of two aksharas, 73.
Dudi ... A kind of drum, 122.
Dūṇ ... A very quick speed, Allegretto, 78. A melody in the same, northern.
Durt ... Allegro time, northern, 78.
Dundubhi ... Ancient name for the nagāra drum, 8, 28
Dvitīya ... Second note of Sāman scale, 27, 30.

Edaka ... Small metal drum, 122.
Ekatāla ... A single beat time-measure, 75, 76.
Esrāj ... Stringed instrument, Bengal, 109.

Farodast ... Four-beat time-measure, northern, 76.
Fillagorī ... A flute, 116.

Gabgūki ... Primitive bow instrument, 115.
Gamaka ... Graces and ornaments, 83, 130.
Gāndhāra ... Third note of the octave, 3, 33.
Gāndhāra grāma ... An ancient scale starting on Ga, 34, 35.
Gāndhārī ... An ancient rāga.
Gandharva ... Class of heavenly musicians.
Gāndharva veda ... Science of music.
Ghasīt ... The slide, 54.
Ghazal ... Form of northern melody, 90.
Gīta Govinda ... An old song on Kṛishṇa, 14.
Gopichand ... Primitive bamboo instrument, 115.
Graha ... The proper starting note for a rāga, 39.
Grāma .. ... An ancient scale, 2, 33.
Guru ... A time beat of eight aksharas, 73.

Humpitam ... A gamaka. Appogiatura, 84.
Harikathā ... Religious musical entertainment, 91.
Horī ... Song of Holi festival, northern, 89.

Ili ... Ancient Tamil name for Pa, 32.

Jalatarang ... A musical instrument of cups, 119.
Jālrā ... Small hand cymbals, 123.
Janaka rāga ... Original rāga, 18.
Janya rāga ... Derivative rāga, 18.
Jhārīgha ... .. Large cymbals, 123.
Jāru ... A slide, 84.
Jāti ... Ancient name for rāga, 2, 10, 42 A class of time-measures, 75.
Javādi ... A Kanarese song, 92.
Jhampa ... A three-beat time, southern, 75. A four-beat time, northern, 76.
Jhārā ... Rapid arpeggio, 85.
Jinjīvi ... Snake charmer's pipe, 118.
Joru ... Medium speed, northern, 78.

Kaikkilai ...	... Ancient Tamil name of Ga, 32.
Kaiśiki ...	... A sharp of Ni, southern, 3, 5.
Kaitāla ...	... Hand cymbals, 71, 123.
Kākali ...	... Highest sharp of Ni, southern, 3, 5.
Kākapāda ...	... Time-beat of sixteen aksharas, 73.
Kāla ...	... Musical speed, 78.
Kalai ...	... A minute division of the akshara, 77.
Kalahāy ...	... A horn, 116.
Kālakshepa	... Musical and religious performance, 91.
Kampitam-Kampa...	The tremolo, 84.
Karadivādya	... Large form of hour-glass drum, 123.
Karadsamila	... Large drum, 122.
Karaṇa ...	... Trumpet, 119.
Karkhā ...	... Rajput war song, 92.
Kartāl ...	... Castanets, 71, 124.
Kā-sharati	... A flute, 117.
Kastaraṅg	... Musical instrument of cups, 119.
Kātyāyana vīṇā	... A vīṇā with 100 strings, 99, 113.
Kāvadi sindhu	... Southern folk song, 92.
Kavāli ...	... Tīntāl. Bengal, 76.
Khāli ...	... Silent beat of northern time-measure, 76.
Khaṇḍa ...	... Jāti of time-measure, southern, 75.
Khañjeri ...	... Form of tambourine, 123.
Khattalā ...	... Castanets, 124.
Khyāl ...	... Northern form of song, 87, 89.
Kinnara ...	... Class of heavenly musicians, 7.
Kinnarī ...	... Primitive stringed instrument, 100, 111, 115.
Kīrtan ...	... Form of musical performance, northern, 91.
Kīrtana ...	... A southern form of melody, 22, 87.
Komal ...	... A flat, 4.
Kombu ...	... Horn, 116.
Komiki ...	... Horn, 116.
Koṭṭuvādyam	... Kind of Tambūr, southern, 111.
Kṛiti ...	... A southern form of melody, 22, 87.
Krushṭa ...	... Highest note of Sāman scale, 27, 30.
Kuma ...	... A sacred trumpet, 118.
Kural ...	... Ancient Tamil name for Sa, 32.
Kuṛal (*Kushal*)	... Panpipe, southern, 119.
Kustar ...	... Castanets, 124.
Laghu ...	... A time-length of four aksharas, 73.
Līnam ...	... A slide, 85.
Madhya ...	... Medium speed, moderato, 78. Middle voice register, 4.
Madhyama	... Fourth note of the octave, 3, 33. Name of an ancient grāma, 34.
Mahānagāra	... A very large nagāra drum, 121.
Mandaran	... Second string of vīṇā, 104.

Mandra ... ... The lower voice register, 4.
Fifth note of the Sāman scale, 27, 30.
Mandragati ... Lower tetrachord of octave.
Mañjīva ... ... Cymbals, 123.
Mārsīya ... ... Hindusthani songs for the Muharram, 90.
Mātra ... ... Unit of time-measure, 12, 71.
Mardala ... ... Mṛidaṅga, southern name, 120.
Maṭhya ... ... Three-beat time-measure, southern, 75.
Mayūri ... ... A peacock dilruba, 114.
Melakarta ... A primary rāga, southern, 19, 42.
Mīnd ... ... The shake, 84.
Mirtāy ... ... Principal time-beat of Āvarta, southern, 76.
Miśra ... ... The seven-member jāti of time-measure, southern, 75.
Mṛidaṅga ... ... A concert drum, southern, 9, 78, 120.
Muralī ... ... A flute, 28, 101, 116.
Mūrchhanā ... Ancient name for modes, 40.
Melody-form for rāga, southern, 85.
A grace note, northern, 85.
Miy ... ... A flute, 117.

Nafari ... ... Small trumpet, 119.
Nagāra ... ... Large kettle drum, 121.
Nagarkīrtan ... A musical and religious performance, 93.
Nāgasara ... ... A clarionet, 117.
Nahabet ... ... A large nagāra, 121.
Nakkāra ... ... Same as nagāra, 121.
Nallatarang ... A pipe instrument, 118.
Nandin ... ... Primitive bamboo instrument, 115.
Nāṭaka ... ... Dramatic performance, 92.
Nāṭya ... ... Music and dancing, 12.
Nīcha ... ... Lower voice register in Sāman chant, 28.
Nidhana ... ... Final section of Sāman chant.
Nidukku ... ... Small drum, 122.
Ninkairna ... Small nāgasara, 117.
Nishādha ... ... Seventh note of octave, 3, 30, 33.
Noṇḍi Sindhu ... Southern folk song, 92.
Nosbug ... ... Drone instrument, 118.
Nyāsa ... ... Proper final note for rāga, 39.

Oḍava ... ... Pentatonic rāga, 46.
Orikai ... ... The shake, 84.
Ovis ... ... Marāṭha song, 92.

Pakhawāj ... ... Large mṛidaṇga northern, 121.
Pakka-sāraṇī ... Side strings of vīṇā, 104.
Pālai ... ... Ancient Dravidian mode, 12, 34.
Pallavi ... ... First section of southern melody. **Chorus**, 87, 88.

Paṇ ... ... Ancient Tamil melody, 12.
Pañchama ... Fifth note of octave, 3, 30, 33.
Second string of vīṇā, 104.
Pañchamā ... A rāga, 54, 56, 69.
Paran ... ... Drum-like stroke on a stringed instrument, 85.
Parand ... ... Particular kind of drum-beat.
Paṭ ... ... A Gamaka, staccato, 85.
Penna ... ... Primitive two-stringed instrument, 112.
Pinaka ... ... Primitive single stringed instrument, 100.
Pluta ... ... Time-measure of twelve aksharas, 73.
Poṅgi ... ... The drone instrument, 118.
Povāda ... ... Marāṭhī war song, 92.
Prabhandha ... Ancient name of musical composition, 14, 87.
Prasaya ... ... Drone note of Sāman chant.
Prastāva ... ... Introductory portion of Sāman chant.
Prathama ... First note of Sāman scale, 27, 30.
Pratihāra ... Second section of Sāman chant.
Pratimadhyama ... Sharpened Ma, southern, 35.
Puñji ... ... Snake charmer's instrument, 101, 118.
Putra ... ... Secondary rāga, northern, 41.
Pūrvāṅga ... ... First tetrachord of octave, 63.

Qanūn ... ... Same as svaramaṇḍala. Persian, 99, 114.

Rabāb ... ... A stringed instrument, 100, 112, 113.
Rabanāstra ... Ancient musical instrument of Rāvaṇa, 100.
Rāga ... ... A melody-type, 2, 10, 39.
Rāg Ālāp ... ... First section of Ālāphana, northern, 86.
Rāgiṇī ... ... Secondary rāga, northern, 41.
Rāgmālā ... ... Same as rāgamālikā, 91.
Rāgamālikā ... Musical composition of many rāgas, 91.
Rishabha ... ... Second note of octave, 3, 30, 33.
Rūpaka ... ... Two-beat time measure, southern, 75.
Three-beat time measure, northern, 76.
Rūpaka Ālāp ... Second section of Ālāphana, northern, 86.

Sādhāraṇa ... Name of first sharp of Ga, southern, 3, 5.
Sādras ... ... A Hindusthani melody, 89.
Sam ... ... Principal beat of a time section, northern, 76.
Sāman ... ... Chants of ancient Sāma Veda, 27.
Sampūrṇa ... Rāga containing all the notes of the octave in both ascent and descent, 42.
Saṁvādī ... Perfect consonance, 25, 26.
Saṁvāditva ... Theory of consonance, 26.
Sanāi ... ... A trumpet, 119.
Sañchārī ... ... Third section of northern melody, 87.
Ascent and descent of octave, 39.
Sandhiprakāś ... Morning and evening twilight. Name given to rāgas to be sung at that time, 63.

Saṅgati ... ... Variations of theme, 22, 88.
Śaṅkhu ... ... Conch shell, 99, 116.
Saṅkīrṇa ... ... Seven-member jāti of time-measure, southern, 75.
Saṅkīrtan ... Musical performance, 93.
Saptaka ... ... The seven notes of the gamut, 30.
Sāraṇī ... ... First string of vīṇā, 104.
Sāraṅgī ... ... A stringed instrument, Indian violin, 100, 108.
Sarasvatī ... ... Goddess of music and arts, 7.
Name of particular kind of vīṇā.
Sargam ... ... A song in sol-fa syllables, 90.
Sārindā ... ... A variety of Sāraṅgī, 109.
Sāroda ... ... A form of Sāraṅgī, 100, 109.
Sarrawat ... ... Kind of Sāraṅgī, 109.
Satār ... ... Same as sitār.
Śata-tantrī-vīṇā ... A vīṇā with 100 strings, 99, 113.
Shāḍava ... ... Hexatonic rāga, 46.
Shaḍja ... ... First note of the octave, 3, 30, 33.
The name of an ancient grāma, 34.
Shaṭkāla ... ... Sextuple time, 73.
Shaṭśruti ... ... Name given to sharps of Ri and Dha, southern, 3, 5.
Siṁhanandana ... An intricate southern time-measure, 77.
Sindhu ... ... Southern folk melody, 92.
Sitār ... ... A stringed instrument, 15, 105 sq.
Sphuritam ... The shake, 84.
Śringa ... ... Horn, 116.
Śruti ... ... Enharmonic interval or note, 2, 5, 18, 26, 29, 37
Śruti Upāṅga ... Drone instrument, 118.
Sthāyī ... ... A voice register.
Śuddha ... ... Natural diatonic scale and notes, 2, 36.
Sūkth ... ... Same as Jāru, slide, 84.
Sūlaphākatā ... A three-beat time measure, northern, 76
Sundarī ... ... The sitār, 107.
Sūntha ... ... Same as Jāru, slide, 84.
Surbahār ... ... A stringed instrument, Bengal, 108.
Surnāī ... ... The nāgasara, northern.
Surphākatā ... A three-beat time measure, northern, 76.
Sūr-śriṅgāra ... A stringed instrument, 113.
Sursota ... ... A variety of tambūr, 111.
Svara ... ... Diatonic interval or note, 2, 30, 32.
Svaramālikā ... Portion of song in sol-fa syllables, 90.
Svaramaṇḍala ... A stringed instrument like dulcimer, 113.
Svàrasāhityā ... A portion of song in sol-fa syllables, 90.
Svarāvarta ... A portion of song in sol-fa syllables, 90.
Śvarita ... ... A falling accent in Saman chant, 27, 30.
Tabla ... ... Pair of small drums, 78, 120.
Tāla ... ... Time-measure, 2, 72.

Tambūr ... ... A stringed instrument, 100, 110.
Tappā ... ... A Hindusthani melody, 20, 89.
Tāra ... ... Higher voice register, 4.
Tāram ... ... Ancient Tamil name for Ni, 32.
Tarāna ... ... Form of song, 99.
Tatūri ... ... Trumpet, 119.
Taush ... ... Peacock Dilruba, 114.
Tenmāṅgu ... Southern folk melody, 92.
Thambatti ... Tambourine, 123.
Thantona ... ... Primitive bamboo instrument, 115.
Thāṭ ... ... Melody-type, northern, 40.
Theka ... ... Drum phrases.
Thoṅk ... ... A gamaka, staccato, 85.
Thumri ... ... Hindusthani love song, 89.
Tillāna ... ... Form of song, 90.
Tīntāl ... ... Same as Tītāla, 76.
Tītāla ... ... Three-beat time, northern, 76.
Tīvra ... ... A sharpened note, 4.
Tīvratama ... Slight further sharpening of **Tīvratara**, 4.
Tīvratara ... ... A double sharp, 4.
Tombi ... ... Snake charmer's instrument, 118.
Tomtom ... ... A drum, 123.
Tripuṭa ... ... Three-beat time, southern, 75.
Trisra ... ... Three-akshara Jāti of southern time-measure 75.
Tritāl ... ... Same as Tītāla, 76.
Tritīya ... ... Third note of Sāman scale, 27, 30.
Trivata ... ... A form of song, 90.
Turahi ... ... A trumpet, 119.
Tuttam ... ... Ancient Tamil name for Ri, 32.
Tsauṅg ... ... Primitive bamboo instrument, 115.

Uchcha ... ... Higher notes of Sāman chant, 28.
Udātta ... ... Raised tone of Sāman, 27.
Udgītha ... ... Second section of Sāman chant.
Udukku ... ... Hour-glass drum, 122.
Udupe ... ... Goblet shaped drum, 123.
Uḷai ... ... Ancient Tamil name for Ma, 32.
Upadrava ... ... Fourth section of Sāman chant.
Uttara rāga ... Rāga with aṁśa in Uttarāṅga, 63.
Uttarāṅga ... Higher tetrachord of octave, 63.

Vādī ... ... Principal note of a rāga, aṁśa, 25, 26.
Vaṅśa ... ... A flute, 116.
Varek ... ... Shake. A Gamaka, 84.
Varja ... ... Omitted notes in a rāga.
Varṇa ... ... Variations of a melody, 88.
Vibhāga ... ... A bar in time-measure, 6, 74.
Vikrit ... ... **One of the śrutis—chromatic variation of diatonic note, 2.**

Vilamba ...	... Slow speed, adagio, southern, 78.
Vilari ...	... Ancient Tamil name for Dha, 32.
Vinavah ...	... Ancient one-stringed instrument of Ceylor. 100.
Vīṇā ...	... A stringed instrument, 7, 8, 10, 11, 18, 28, 101 sq.
Virāṃa ...	... Rest in time-measure, 74.
Visāragīti...	... Ancient style of singing, 89.
Vivādī ...	... A dissonant note, 26.
Yāḷ (Yāzh)	... Ancient Tamil instument, 11.
Yektār ...	... A one-stringed instrument, 112.
Zamzamma	... Very rapid arpeggio, 84.

APPENDIX III

EXAMPLES OF INDIAN MUSIC

The following points should be noted in regard to the notation below:

A superscript small letter indicates an Appogiatura note: as mG

D.C. indicates a repeat from the beginning.

Fine indicates that after the repeat the melody ends at that place.

$ means that a phrase is repeated beginning at the place marked thus.

In regard to time-signature, the Āvarta is shown by two upright strokes, thus ||

The bar is shown by one stroke, thus |

The beats in the bar, by short strokes are shown thus ¦

The divisions of the beat are shown by two dots, thus :

For explanation of other signs see Introduction.

In some of the melodies the rāga outline, or chhāyā as it is called, is given with a time-bar.

I Sāman Chants

Sung by Sundara Rāgavachār, Triplicane, Madras.

No. 1. Invocation to Indra.

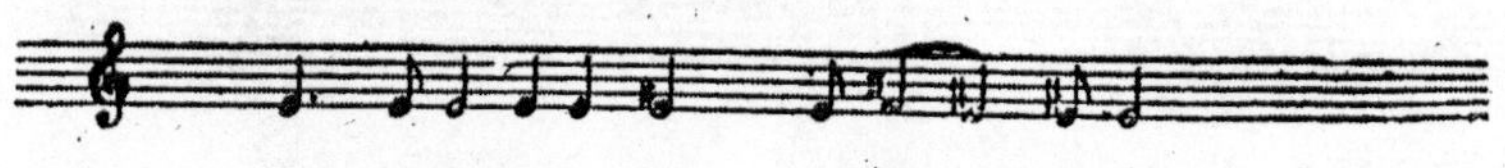

A . . bhi tvā śu-ra-no nu-mo. . dugdhā

i-va de-na-va- ṛ ha I - • śā na-mas- ya

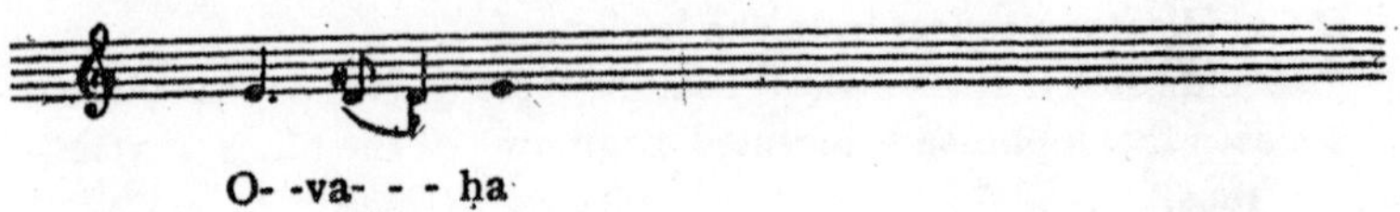

No. 2. Another.

II The Lyre of the Universe

From Sir Rabindranath Tagore (with Bengālī words)

Mixed rāga *Chāpu and Eka tāla*

Astāī

||G:-:G:G:-|MG:R:S:-:-||G:G:M:P:-|D:n:D:n:-||^{n}D:P:M:P:-|P:D:n:Ṡ:-||

Biś-wabī- ṇārabe -.-biśwajan- mohichche- - - - - - - - - -

Fine.

||P:D:n:Ṡ:- |n:D:P:D:-||P:D:Ṡ:nD:P|D:n:D:P: ||PD:nn:PP:-:G|M:-:-:-:- ||

Sthale jale nabhatale bane upabane, Nadī nade giriguhā pārābā-re.

Antarā

||^{P}N:N:N:Ṡ:-|^{N}Ṡ:P:P:P:-||P:D:P:M:P:-|M|G:-:-:-||R:G:P:M:GR|SN:D:ND:P:-||

Nitya jāge saras saṅ-gīt madhu - rimā, Nitya nṛityaras bhaṅgimā.

Sañchārī *Eka tāla*

||^{P}N:N:N:-|N:DN:P:P||DP:M:PM:G:-| -:MG:R:GG||

Āshāre naba ānanda utsab naba. Atigambhīr

||-:MG:R:GG |-:-:-:GP||M:G:G:RR|SN:S:-:- ||

Atigambhīr nīl ambaredamaru bāje,

‖N̲:S:S:-|-:-:-:N̲S ‖S:RR:G:GR:|R:S:-:-N̲S‖N:NN:D:NS̄ S̄S̄:S̄:S̄:-‖

Jenare pralayaṅkarī saṅkarī nāche, Kare garjjan nirjharinī saghane,

‖-:S̄S̄:S̄:R̄:S̄ |N:S̄N:D:ND‖P:DP:M:PM|G:MG:R:G‖RG:MP:MG:RR|R:-:S:-‖

Hera kshubdha bhavāl biśāl nirāl piyāl tamāl Uthe raba bhairab tāne. bitāne.

‖NN:NN:N:-N|N:N:DN:N‖-:-:N:NN DN:S̄:-:- ‖

Paban mallārgīta gāhichche āndhār rāte ;

‖R̄:-R̄:RS̄:- N:-N:S̄S̄:- ‖NS̄:-S̄:S̄N:- |D:-D:ND:-‖P:PD:P:-M|G:-:-:- ‖

Unmādinī sodāminī rangabhare nṛitya kare ambarta - le.

‖SR:SR:GR:-N̲ S:-:-:- ‖SR:GM:PD:N|S̄:-:-:- ‖S̄N:DP:MG:R|S:-:-:-‖

Dikedike katabāṇī nabanaba katabhāsha jhar jhar rasadhārā

N.B.—A final consonant in above is pronounced as though it had a short *a* sound following it. Thus jhar jhar is pronounced *jhara jhara*.

Sir Rabindranath Tagore was good enough to allow me to take down this song from his own singing, for which I am very grateful.

THE LYRE OF THE UNIVERSE

(TRANSLATION OF THE BENGĀLĪ)

With the music of the lyre of the universe humanity is charmed. Whether on land or water or under the sky, in the forest or the glade, in the river and streams, in the mountain and cave and in the ocean, sweet music's charm is always awake. It is always dancing playfulness; in the rainy month there is new joy and festivals new; in the blue sky the drum of Siva is played as if the destructive goddess is dancing. The rivulets roar loudly and the groves of lonely mighty trees are awed and frightened; sound rises with a terrible noise; the breeze sings the mallār rāga on a dark night; mad lightnings dance with coyness under the heavens; on every side there are new words, new languages, rippling streams of water.

III PUNJĀBĪ TUNES

Astāī $ — 1. Psalm 24 — *Fine*

‖S:S:S:G:-:G¦M:-:M:P:-:-¦Ṡ:-:n:D:-:P|M:-:M:G:-:R S:S:S:G:-:G¦M:-:M:P:-‖

Rabb Khudāwand Bādshāh hai, oh jalāl dā Bādshāh hai, Rabb
Khudāwand Bādshāh hai

Antarā

‖M:-:M:N:-:N¦N:-:N:Ṡ:-:Ṡ Ṡ:-:Ṡ:Ṡ:-:Ṙ Ṡ:-:n:D:-:P

Uchche karo, sir, darwāzo, uchche ho sab daro;

D.C.

‖N:-:N:Ṡ:-:Ṙ ¦Ṡ:-:n:D:P:D ¦Ṡ:-:n:D:-:P|M:-:-:G:-:R‖

Jān jalāl dā Bādshāh āwe, sir tad uchche karo.

N.B.—*The Indian notation under the staff in the first line of this song cannot come directly under the corresponding notes in the staff on account of lack of space.*

2. Psalm 86

$ *Fine*

‖PP:PP:PM:M¦gg:RS:R-g:R‖nS:SS:RR:R¦RP:PP:M-g:R‖

Ai Khudāwand, āpnī rāh āpne
bande nūn wikhā
Terī hī sachiai di, Karūṅga
maiṇ parāwī

D.C.

‖nn:nn:nn:Ṡ¦DD:PM:PP:P‖

Merā dīl ik pāse kar Tān maiṇ rakkhān terā ḍar

3. Psalm 111

$ *Astāi* *Fine* D.C.

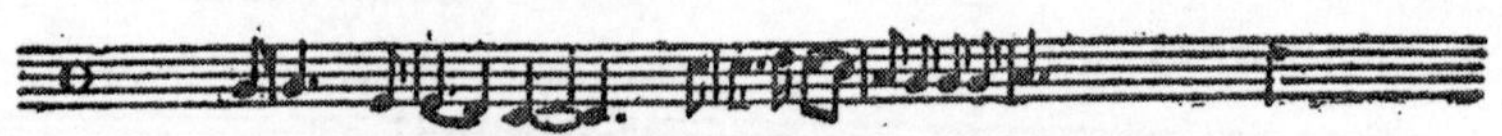

P¦P:-:-:G¦G:R:S:-¦-:-:-Ṡ¦Ṡ:-Ṙ:Ṡ:N¦D:P:P:P¦D:-:-

Tu-sī gā-o sanā, gāo sanātusi Rabb dī

Antarā D.C.

P¦P:D:Ṡ:Ṡ¦Ṡ:Ṡ-:Ṙ¦Ṙ:Ṙ:Ṡ:-¦N:-:D:P¦D:Ṙ:Ṡ:N¦D:P:P:P¦D:-:-

Sachcheān dī tolī wich dil nāl gawān Sanā sunāwan main Rabb dī

IV Hindusthani Melodies.

(From Collection of Mr. N. V. Bhātkhande)

No. 1

Mālsarī rāga *Sūlphākatā tāla*

The above is the rāga and its characteristic phrase.

$ *Astāi* *Fine*

Antarā D.C.

No. 2

Bilāval *Tīntāl*

S R G M P D n‾ N S̄ S:G:P:M|G:R|G:R|

The above is the rāga and its characteristic phrase.

|:-:-.S:GP|MG:RS|GP:n‾N|S̄:NS̄:-.S̄:DP|MG:RS|GP:n‾N‖

‖S̄:NS̄:-.S̄:NS̄|ĠR̄:ĠM̄|ĠR̄:S̄N|S̄Ġ:R̄S̄:DN:DP|n‾M:GR|GP:n‾N‖S̄:NS̄:-.

No. 3

Yamankalyānī rāga *Tritāla*

S R G m P D n‾N S ‖S:R:G:m|P:D:N:S̄|S̄:N:D:P|m:G:R:S‖

Astāi

‖mP:N:D:N|m:P:m:G|mP:-:P:Dm|-:mG:G:-‖

||^{m}G:^{m}G:R:G|m:^{G}m:P:P|G:R:G:R|^{N}S:R:S:-||

||^{m}S:S:R:R|G:G:m:^{G}m|P:-:P:^{N}Ṡ|N:^{D}N:m:P||

Antarā

||^{p}G:-:G:P|-:P:D:P|^{p}Ṡ:-:Ṡ:^{N}Ṡ|-:Ṙ:Ṡ:-||

||^{s}D:-:D:Ṡ|-:Ṡ:Ṡ:-|^{N}Ṡ:Ṙ:Ġ:Ṙ|^{N}Ṡ:N:n^{-}:P||

||^{m}P:-:P:P|^{D}m:m:G:R|G:R:G:R|^{N}S:R:S:-||

||S:R^{-}:G:m|P:D:N:Ṡ|N:D:P:m|G:R^{-}:S:-||

N.B. *F♯ has been omitted by error from the stave in the above four lines.*

V Carnatic Melodies.

1. Song of Tāyumānavar.

With Tamil words and rough English alliterative translation.

Nādanāmakriyā rāga *Eka tāla*

S r M G M P d N Ṡ Ṡ N d P M G r s |s:r:M:-|

Fine

|S:r:M:- | M:M:M:- || M:M:G:M | G̃:-:-:- ||

Ponnai mā-tarai Bhū-mi-yai nādi-den . . . . . .

Gold or land, yea or plea-sures. I seek no more.

||G:M:d:- | P:M:GM:PM: | GM:PM:GM:Gr | S:-:-:- ||

Yennai nā-di-ya yen uyir nā-tha-ne - - - - - - - - - - - -

Sealed for Thee is my life, Seeker of my soul!

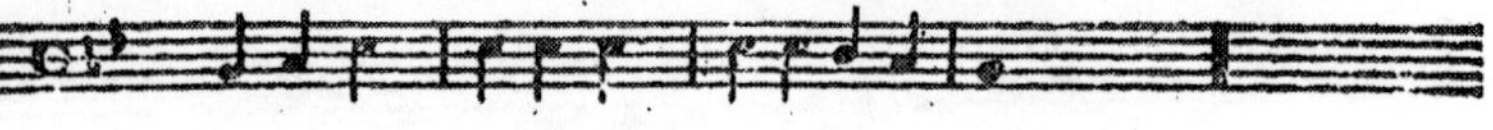

||P:d:Ṡ:- | Ṡ:Ṡ:Ṡ:- Ṡ:Ṡ:N:d | P:-:-:- ||

Unnai nā-duvan un-naruḷ tū-ve-ḷi

Boldly Thee do I seek and thy boundless grace

D.C.

||G:M:d:- | P:M:GM:PM GM:PM:GM:Gr | S:-:-:- ||

Tannai nā-duvan tannan ṭan-ni-ya-nē - - - - - - -

Holding Thee all-supreme, hungry I seek for thee.

2. An Old Melody.

D.C.

|PP:DP|MG GR|GP:MG RS|RG||

Ch. III.

||PP:P|RR|R|GPMG:G GP|MG|GPMG:MGRS|RSRG|S|RS:ND|S|-||

D.C.

||MGRG:P|DPDR|S|RS:ND PM|GR||

No. 3

From *Oriental Music in Staff Notation.*

Sindhurāmakriyā rāga *Deśādi tāla*

4 2 2

SGMPdNSSNPdPMGS |MP:MM|G|G|

Pallavi.

N|S:G|-|M|P:-|-|d|P:P|-|M|MG:G|S|N|S:G|-|M|Pd:Nd|N|P|d:P|-|M|MG:G|
S|S|

Fine

|N:N|P|d|NS:G|-|G|G:GM|P|M||MP:MM|G|G|S:G|-|M|Pd:Nd|N|P|d:P|-|M||

MG:G|-|-|S:-|-||

Anupallavi.

P|d:N|-|S|N:S|-|SN|S:-|-N||-:Pd|PM|P|d:N|-|S|N:S|-|N|S:G|-|M||G:G|M|GS||

D.C.

|N:N|P|d|NS:GS|N|S|SN:P|d|dP||MP:MM|G|

Charanam.

P|P:P|-|M|dP:PM|M|G|M:MG|G|S||G:G|-:MP|dN:NP|-|d|PM:MG:S|NP|d:
N|-|S||G:G|-|P|

D.C.

d:N|-|S|N:S|-|N|S:G|-:M||G:G|M|GS|N:N|P|d|NS:GS|N|S|SN:P|d|dP||MP:
MM|G|

No. 4 A Melody of Tyāgarāja.

From *Oriental Music in Staff Notation.*

Madhyamāvatī rāga. *Rūpaka tāla*

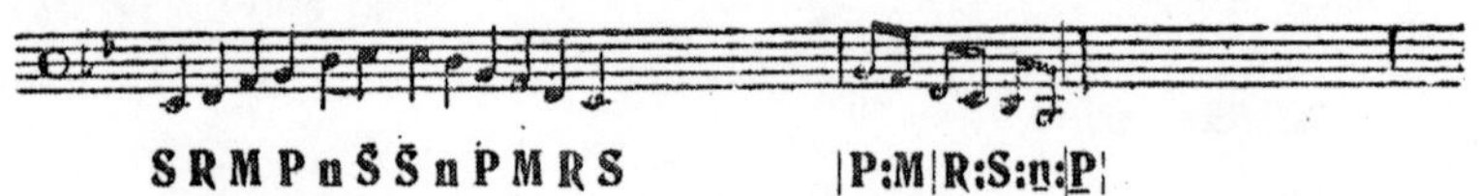

S R M P n Ṡ Ṡ n P M R S |P:M|R:S:n:P|

Pallavi

|P:M|R:S:n:P|R:-|R:R:R:R||nS:RS|RM:RS:n:P|R:-|R:R:R:R||

||P:M|R:PM:RS:nP|R:-|R:R:R:S|RM:-R|MP:-M:Pn:P|P:-|-:-:-:-||

||P:M|R:PM:RS:nP|R:-:R:R:R:S|SR:MR|RM:PM:M:Pn|PM:RM|Pn:PM:R:R||

|P:M|R:PM:RS:nP|R:-|R:R:R:S|SR:MR|RM:PM:Pn:SR|MR:Sn|Sn:PM:R:R|

Fine

‖P:M|R:PM:RS:nP|R:-|R:R:R:S|S:-n|R:-S:S:|S:-|-:-:-:-‖

Anupallavi

‖R:R|R:R:-:R|S:RM|R:-S:S:-n|n:-|nS:R:Sn:P|n:-|S:-:-:-‖

D.C.

‖R:R|R:R:-:R|S:RM|R:-:S:-|n:SR|S:RS:n:Sn|Pn:S|Pn:Sn:PM:R‖

Charanam

‖P:M|P:R:M:R|P:M P:M:R:R|nn:P|nn:M:P:M|RM:P|M:P:P:P‖R:R|R:-:R|

I II D.C.

|S:RM|R:R:R:S|n:SR|S:RS:n:Sn|Pn:S|S:-:-:-‖Pn:S|Pn:Sn:PM:R‖

No. 5

From *Oriental Music in Staff Notation.*

Ānandabhairavī raga. *Trisra Eka tāla*

3

S g R g M P D P n Ṡ Ṡ n D P M g R S | Ṡg:Rg:gM |

Pallavi

|P:PP:-P|P:Pn.n:PM|g^{M}g:M.DP:PM|gg:RS:Sn||Sg:Mg:^{M}gM|gM.P:Mg:RM|

Fine

|gR:g^{M}g:-|Mg.MD:PM.gR:Sn||Sg:Rg:^{M}gM|gM:P:Mg:RM|gR:ggS:-||

Anupallavi

||Sg:RS:-n|nn:nS:SS|Sg:Rg:^{M}gM|MD.P:Mg:^{M}gM||P:PṠ:-Ṡ|nṠ.n:DP:PM|

D.C.

|g^{M}g:M.DP:PM|g^{M}g:RG:gM||

Charanam

‖P:PP:-P|MP.DP:PD.Pn:PM|Mg.g:M.DP:PM|Mg.g:R.RS:Sn‖Sg:Rg:^{M}gM|

|gM.PD:PM.g:RM|gR:g.gg:gS‖Sg:RS:-n|n.Sn:nn.S:-S|Sg:Rg:^{M}gM|

D.C.

gM.PD:PM.MG:GM‖PP:PP:SS|nS.RS:nD.PD:PM|g^{M}g:M.D:PM|Mg.g:
RG:gM‖

No. 6 SOUTHERN FOLK SONG

From *Oriental Music in Staff Notation*.

Ānandakalippu. *Chāpu tāla*

Fine

‖G:M:-:P:-:M:-|G:M:-:G:-:r | S:-:-:S:-:-:-‖ -:-:-:S:-:S:-

D.C.

|M:M:-:M:-:M:-|M:M:-:M:-:M:-‖G:M:-:G:-:r:-|S:r:-:^{r}G:-:-:-‖

D.C.

GENERAL INDEX

(See Glossary for Index to Technical Terms)

INDEX TO RĀGAS

INDEX TO TĀLAS

35. **The Ragas of Hindustan** by the Philharmonic Society of Western India, Poona. 1918. pp. 41, 44. Ayabhushan Press, Poona.

The sarigamas of 79 ragas collected and arranged in an adaptation of the western staff notation. With an Introduction on the Theory of Indian Music by Mr. E. C. Clements, I.C.S. A very useful book.

THE MUSIC OF INDIA

Music has been a cultivated art in India for at least three thousand years. The chant is an essential element of Vedic ritual; and the references in later Vedic literature, the scriptures of Buddhism, and the Brahmanical epics show that it was already highly developed as a secular art in centuries preceding the beginning of the Christian era. Its zenith may perhaps be assigned to the Imperial age of the Guptas—from the fourth to the sixth century A. D. This was the classic period of Sanskrit literature, culminating in the drama of Kalidasa; and to the same time is assigned the monumental treatise of Bharata on the theory of music and drama.

The art music of the present day is a direct descendant of these ancient schools, whose traditions have been handed down with comment and expansion in the guilds of the hereditary musicians. While the words of a song may have been composed at any date, the musical themes communicated orally from master to disciple are essentially ancient. As in other arts and in life, so here also India presents to us the wonderful spectacle of the still surviving consciousness of the ancient world, with a range of emotional experience rarely accessible to those who are preoccupied with the activities of over-production, and intimidated by the economic insecurity of a social order based on competition.

The art music of India exists only under cultivated patronage, and in its own intimate environment. It corresponds to all that is most classical in the European tradition. It is the chamber-music of an aristocratic society, where the patron retains musicians for his own entertainment and for the pleasure of the circle of his friends: or it is temple music, where the musician is the servant of God. The public concert is unknown, and the livelihood of the artist does not depend upon his ability and will to amuse the crowd. In other words, the musician is protected. Under these circumstances he is under no temptation to be anything but a musician; his education begins in infancy, and his art remains a vocation. The civilizations of Asia do not afford to the inefficient amateur those opportunities of self-expression which are so highly appreciated in Europe and America. The arts are nowhere taught as a social accomplishment; on the one hand there is the professional, proficient in a traditional art, and on the other the lay public. The musical cultivation of the public does not consist in "everybody doing it," but in appreciation and reverence.

I have indeed heard the strange objection raised that to sing the music of India one must be an artist; and this objection seems to voice a typically democratic disapproval of superiority. But it would be nearly as true to say that the listener must respond with an art of his own, and this would be entirely in accord with Indian theories of æsthetic. The musician in India finds a model audience—technically critical, but somewhat indifferent to voice production. The Indian audience listens rather to the song than to the singing of the song: those who are musical, perfect the rendering of the song by the force of their own imagination and emotion. Under these conditions the actual music is better heard than where the sensuous perfection of the voice is made a *sine qua non*: precisely as the best sculpture is primitive rather than suave, and we prefer conviction to prettiness—"It is like the outward poverty of God,[1] whereby His glory is nakedly revealed." None the less the Indian singer's voice is sometimes of great intrinsic beauty, and sometimes used with sensitive intelligence as well as skill. It is not, however, the voice that makes the singer, as so often happens in Europe.

Since Indian music is not written, and cannot be learnt from books, except in theory, it will be understood that the only way for a foreigner to learn it must be to establish between himself and his Indian teachers that special relationship of disciple and master which belongs to Indian education in all its phases: he must enter into the inner spirit and must adopt many of the outer conventions of Indian life, and his study must continue until he can improvise the songs under Indian conditions and to the satisfaction of Indian professional listeners. He must possess not only the imagination of an artist, but also a vivid memory and an ear sensitive to microtonal inflections.

The theory of scale is everywhere a generalisation from the facts of song. The European art scale has been reduced to twelve fixed notes by merging nearly identical intervals such as D sharp and E flat, and it is also tempered to facilitate modulation and free change of key. In other words, the piano is out of tune by hypothesis. Only this compromise, necessitated in the development of harmony, has made possible the triumphs of modern orchestration. A purely melodic art, however, may be no less intensely cultivated, and retains the advantages of pure intonation and modal colouring.

Apart from the keyed instruments of modern Europe there scarcely exists an absolutely fixed scale: at any rate, in India the thing fixed is a group of intervals, and the precise vibration value of a note depends on its position in a progression. not on its relation to a tonic. The scale of twenty-two notes is simply the sum of all the notes used in all the songs—no musician sings a chromatic scale from C to C with twenty-two stopping places, for this would be a mere *tour de force*.

The 'quarter-tone' or *shruti* is the microtonal interval between two successive scale notes: but as the theme rarely employes two and never three scale notes in succession, the microtonal interval is not generally conspicuous except in ornament.

Every Indian song is said to be in a particular *raga or ragini*—ragini being the feminine of raga, and indicating an abridgement or modification of the main theme. The raga, like the old Greek and the ecclesiastical mode, is a selection of five, six, or seven notes, distributed along the scale; but the raga is more particularized than a mode, for it has certain characteristic progressions, and a chief note to which the singer constantly returns. None of the ragas employs more than seven substantive notes, and there is no modulation: the strange tonality of the Indian song is due to the use of unfamiliar intervals, and not to the use of many successive notes with small divisions.

The raga may be best defined as a melody-mould or the ground plan of a song. It is this ground plan which the master first of all communicates to the pupil; and to sing is to improvise upon the theme thus defined. The possible number of ragas is very large, but the majority of systems recognise thirty-six, that is to say six ragas, each with five raginis. The origin of the ragas is various: some, like Pahari, are derived from local folk-song, others, like Jog, from the songs of wandering ascetics, and still others are the creation of great musicians by whose names they are known. More than sixty are mentioned in a Sanskrit-Tibetan vocabulary of the seventh century, with names such as 'With-a-voice-like-a-thunder-cloud,' 'Like-the-god-Indra,' and 'Delighting-the-heart.' Amongst the raga names in modern use may be cited 'Spring,' 'Evening beauty,' 'Honey-flower,' 'The swing,' 'Intoxication.'

Psychologically the word raga, meaning colouring or passion, suggests to Indian ears the idea of mood; that is to say that precisely as in ancient Greece, the musical mode has definite *ethos.* It is not the purpose of the song to repeat the confusion of life, but to express and arouse particular passions of body and soul in man and nature. Each raga is associated with an hour of the day or night when it may be appropriately sung, and some are associated with particular seasons or have definite magic effects. Thus there is still believed the well-known story of a musician whose royal patron arbitrarily insisted on hearing a song in the Dipak raga, which creates fire: the musician obeyed under protest, but as the song proceeded, he burst into flames, which could not be extinguished even though he sprang into the waters of the Jamna. It is just because of this element of magic, and the association of the ragas with the rhythmic ritual of daily and seasonal life, that their clear outlines must not be blurred by modulation: and this is expressed, when the ragas are personified as musical genii, by saying that 'to sing out of the raga' is to break the limbs of these musical angels. A characteristic story is related of the prophet Narada, when he was still but a learner. He thought that he had mastered the whole art of music; but the all-wise Vishnu, to curb his pride, revealed to him in the world of the gods, a spacious building where there lay men and women weeping over their broken arms and legs. They were the ragas and raginis, and they said that a certain sage of the name of Narada, ignorant of music and unskillful in performance, had sung them amiss, and therefore their features were distorted and their limbs broken, and until they were sung truly there would be no cure for them. Then Narada was humbled, and kneeling before Vishnu prayed to be taught the art of music more perfectly: and in due course he became the great musician priest of the gods.

Indian music is a purely melodic art, devoid of any harmonised accompaniment other than a drone. In modern European art, the meaning of each note of the theme is mainly brought out by the notes of the chord which are heard with it; and even in unaccompanied melody, the musician hears an implied harmony. Unaccompanied folk-song does not satisfy the concert-goer's ear; as pure melody it is the province only of the peasant and the specialist. This is partly because the folk-air played on the piano or written in staff notation is actually falsified; but much more because under the conditions of European art, melody no longer exists in its own right, and music is a compromise between melodic freedom and harmonic necessity. To hear the music of India as Indians hear it one must recover the sense of a pure intonation and must forget all implied harmonies. It is just like the effort which we have to make when for the first time, after being accustomed to modern art, we attempt to read the language of early Italian or Chinese painting, where there is expressed with equal economy of means all that intensity of experience which nowadays we are accustomed to understand only through a more involved technique.

Another feature of Indian song—and so also of the instrumental solo—is the elaborate grace. It is natural that in Europe, where many notes are heard simultaneously, grace should appear as an unnecessary elaboration, added to the note, rather than a structural factor. But in India the note and the microtonal grace compose a closer unity, for the grace fulfils just that function of adding light and shade which in harmonised music is attained by the varying degrees of assonance. The Indian song without grace would seem to Indian ears as bald as the European art song without the accompaniment which it presupposes.

Equally distinctive is the constant portamento, or rather, glissando. In India it is far more the interval than the note that is sung or played, and we recognize accordingly a continuity of sound: by contrast with this, the European song, which is vertically divided by the harmonic interest and the nature of the keyed instruments which are heard with the voice, seems to unaccustomed Indian ears to be "full of holes."

All the songs, except the 'alaps' are in strict rhythms. These are only difficult to follow at a first hearing because the Indian rhythms are founded, as in prosody, on contrasts of long and short duration, while European rhythms are based on stress, as in dance or marching. The Indian musician does not mark the beginning of the bar by accent. His fixed unit is a section, or group of bars which are not necessarily alike, while the European fixed unit is typically the bar, of which a varying number constitute a section. The European rhythm is counted in multiples of 2 or 3, the Hindu in sums of 2 or 3. Some of the countings are very elaborate: Ata Tala, for example, is counted as 5 plus 5 plus 2 plus 2. The frequent use of cross rhythms also complicates the form. Indian music is modal in times as well as melody. For all these reasons it is difficult to grasp immediately the point at which a rhythm begins and ends, although this is quite easy for the Indian audience accustomed to quantitative poetic recitation. The best way to approach the Indian rhythm is to pay attention to the phrasing, and ignore pulsation.

The Indian art-song is accompanied by drums, or by the instrument known as a *tambura,* or by both. The tambura is of the lute tribe, but without frets: the four very long strings are tuned to sound the dominant, the upper tonic twice, and the octave below, which are common to all ragas: the pitch is adjusted to suit the singer's voice. The four strings are fitted with simple resonators—shreds of wool between the string and the bridge—which are the source of their 'life': and the strings are continuously sounded, making a pedal point background very rich in overtones, and against this dark ground of infinite potentiality the song stands out like an elaborate embroidery. The tambura must not be regarded ~~as a solo~~ instrument, nor as an object of separate interest like the piano accompaniment of a modern song: its sound is rather the ambient in which the song lives and moves and has its being.

India has, besides the tambura, many solo instruments. By far the most important of these in the *vina*. This classic instrument, which ranks with the violin of Europe and the koto of Japan, and second only to the voice in sensitive response, differs chiefly from the tambura in having frets, the notes being made with the left hand and the strings plucked with the right. The delicate nuances of microtonal grace are obtained by deflection of the strings, whole passages being played in this manner solely by a lateral movement of the left hand, without a fresh plucking. While the only difficulty in playing the tambura is to maintain an even rhythm independently of the song, the *vina* presents all the difficulties of technique that can be imagined, and it is said that at least twelve years are required to attain proficiency.

The Indian singer is a poet, and the poet a singer. The dominant subject matter of the songs is human or divine love in all its aspects, or the direct praise of God, and the words are always sincere and passionate. The more essentially the singer is a musician, however, the more the words are regarded merely as the vehicle of the music: in art-song the words are always brief, voicing a mood rather than telling any story, and they are used to support the music with little regard to their own logic—precisely as the representative element in a modern painting merely serves as the basis for an organisation of pure form or colour. In the musical form called *alap*—an improvisation on the raga theme, this preponderance of the music is carried so far that only meaningless syllables are used. The voice itself is a musical instrument, and the song is more than the words of the song. This form is especially favoured by the Indian virtuoso, who naturally feels a certain contempt for those whose first interest in the song is connected with the words. The voice has thus a higher status than in Europe, for the music exists in its own right and not merely to illustrate the words. Rabindranath Tagore has written on this:

When I was very young I heard the song, 'Who dressed you like a foreigner?', and that one line of the song painted such a strange picture in my mind that even now it is sounding in my memory. I once tried to compose a song myself under the spell of that line. As I hummed the tune, I wrote the first line of the song, 'I know thee, thou stranger,' and if there were no tune to it, I cannot tell what meaning would be left in the song. But by the power of the spell of the tune the mysterious figure of that stranger was evoked in my mind. My heart began to say, 'There is a stranger going to and fro in this world of ours—her house is on the further shore of an ocean of mystery—sometimes she is to be seen in the autumn morning, sometimes in the flowery midnight—sometimes we receive an intimation of her in the depths of our heart—sometimes I hear her voice when I turn my ear to the sky.' The tune of my song led me to the very door of that stranger who ensnares the universe and appears in it, and I said:

'Wandering over the world
I come to thy land:
I am a guest at thy door, thou stranger.'

One day, many days afterwards, there was someone going along the road singing:

'How does that unknown bird go to and away from the cage?
Could I but catch it, I would set the chain of my mind about its feet!'

I saw that that folk-song, too, said the very same thing! Sometimes the unknown bird comes to the closed cage and speaks a word of the limitless unknown—the mind would keep it forever, but cannot. What but the tune of a song could report the coming and going of that unknown bird? Because of this I always feel a hesitation in publishing a book of songs, for in such a book the main thing is left out.

This Indian music is essentially impersonal: it reflects an emotion and an experience which are deeper and wider and older than the emotion or wisdom of any single individual. Its sorrow is without tears, its joy without exultation and it is passionate without any loss of serenity. It is in the deepest sense of the words all-human. But when the Indian prophet speaks of inspiration, it is to say that the Vedas are eternal, and all that the poet achieves by his devotion is to hear or see: it is then Sarasvati, the goddess of speech and learning, or Narada, whose mission it is to disseminate occult knowledge in the sound of the strings of his vina, or Krishna, whose flute is forever calling us to leave the duties of the world and follow Him—it is these, rather than any human individual, who speak through the singer's voice, and are seen in the movements of the dancer.

Or we may say that this is an imitation of the music in heaven. The master musicians of India are always represented as the pupils of a god, or as visiting the heavenworld to learn there the music of the spheres—that is to say, their knowledge springs from a source far within the surface of the empirical activity of the waking consciousness. In this connection it is explained why it is that human art must be studied, and may not be identified with the imitation of our everyday behaviour.[2] When Shiva expounds the technique of the drama to Bharata—the famous author of the *Natya Shastra*—he declares that human art must be subject to law, because in man the inner and outer life are still in conflict. Man has not yet found Himself, but all his activity proceeds from a laborious working of the mind, and all his virtue is self-conscious. What we call our life is uncoördinated, and far from the harmony of art, which rises above good and evil. It is otherwise with the gods, whose every gesture immediately reflects the affections of the inner life. Art is an imitation of that perfect spontaneity—the identity of intuition and expression in those who are of the kingdom of heaven, which is within us. Thus it is that art is nearer to life than any fact can be; and Mr. Yeats has reason when he says that Indian music, though its theory is elaborate and its technique so difficult, is not an art, but life itself.

For it is the inner reality of things, rather than any transient or partial experience that the singer voices. "Those who sing here," says Shankaracharya, "sing God": and the *Vishnu Purana* adds, "All songs are a part of Him, who wears a form of sound."[8] We could deduce from this a metaphysical interpretation of technique. In all art there are monumental and articulate elements, masculine and feminine factors which are unified in perfect form. We have here the sound of the tambura which is heard before the song, during the song, and continues after it: that is the timeless Absolute, which as it was in the beginning, is now and ever shall be. On the other hand there is the song itself which is the variety of Nature, emerging from its source and returning at the close of its cycle. The harmony of that undivided Ground with this intricate Pattern is the unity of Spirit and Matter. We see from this why this music could not be improved by harmonisation, even if harmonisation were possible without destroying the modal bases: for in breaking up the ground into an articulate accompaniment, we should merely create a second melody, another universe, competing with the freedom of the song itself, and we should destroy the peace on which it rests.

This would defeat the purpose of the singer. Here in this ego-conscious world we are subject to mortality. But this mortality is an illusion, and all its truths are relative: over against this world of change and separation there is a timeless and spaceless Peace which is the source and goal of all our being—"that noble Pearl," in the words of Behmen, "which to the World appears Nothing, but to the Children of Wisdom is All Things." Every religious teacher offers us those living waters. But the way is hard and long: we are called upon to leave houses and lands, fathers and mothers and wives to achieve an end which in our imperfect language we can only speak of as Nonexistence. Many of us have great possessions, and the hardest of these to surrender are our own will and identity. What guarantee have we that the reward will be commensurate with the sacrifice?

Indian theory declares that in the ecstasies of love and art we already receive an intimation of that redemption. This is also the *katharsis* of the Greeks, and it is found in the æsthetic of modern Europe when Goethe says

For beauty they have sought in every age
He who perceives it is from himself set free——

aus sich entrückt. We are assured by the experience of æsthetic contemplation that Paradise is a reality.

In other words the magical effects of a song in working mere miracles are far surpassed by its effects upon our inner being. The singer is still a magician, and the song is a ritual, a sacred ceremony, an ordeal which is designed to set at rest that wheel of the imagination and the senses which alone hinder us from contact with reality. But to achieve this ordeal the hearer must coöperate with the musician by the surrender of the will, and by drawing in his restless thought to a single point of concentration: this is not the time or place for curiosity or admiration. Our attitude towards an unknown art should be far from the sentimental or romantic, for it can bring us nothing that we have not already with us in our own hearts: the peace of the Abyss which underlies all art is one and the same, whether we find it in Europe or in Asia.